1 2 3 4 5 6 7 8 9–BC-79 78 77 76 75 74

The Mayor's Mandate

The Mayor's Mandate
Municipal Statecraft
and Political Trust

Ann Greer

SCHENKMAN PUBLISHING COMPANY
Cambridge, Massachusetts

Schenkman books are distributed by
General Learning Press
250 James Street
Morristown, New Jersey 07960

For the mayor, my mother, and Scott

CONTENTS

LIST OF TABLES

ix

ACKNOWLEDGEMENTS

I thank my teachers, Scott Greer and Howard S. Becker, whose thinking did much to shape the direction I have taken in this book. I am grateful also to the other members of the Sociology faculty at Northwestern University and to those faculty members at Lake Forest College who encouraged and assisted me.

I am especially appreciative for the generosity of the long suffering citizens of Waukegan, Illinois who time and time again shared their knowledge and opinions with me. I regret they are too numerous to name. I appreciate the generous cooperation of the Waukegan News-Sun and their reporter, Jack Hagler, whose accurate reporting allowed me considerable extension of my study.

I thank my mother who polled, clipped from the newspaper, edited, criticized, and typed all the versions.

Most of all, I thank Waukegan's extraordinary mayor, Robert S. Sabonjian, for his openness, his fearlessness, and his willingness to share his intelligence.

Introduction

The Mayor's Mandate is a study of the role of the mayor. It is a case study based primarily on observations in Waukegan, Illinois, a northern industrial city. My research into the politics of Waukegan and ultimately into the role of the mayor, has involved a number of approaches, some more and some less systematic. I grew up in Waukegan, graduating from the township high school in 1963. Then I obtained my college and university degrees from institutions in nearby communities, always spending much time in Waukegan and returning there for vacations. My father was a local physician; my mother, a teacher in the public school system. I held various jobs in Waukegan during my high school and college years. All of these circumstances combined to make me aware of life in the community over a considerable time period. When I began more systematic research into the community, I was never refused entrée or an interview and generally found people cooperative and helpful.

My first research in the community was in the early months of 1965. At that time I examined the social characteristics of aldermen elected to the council (plus those candidates defeated) between 1951 and 1965 (later updated to include councils through 1967).[1] In the spring of 1966, I engaged in a large-scale study of reputational influence. I compiled a list of influentials and interviewed at length the eighteen men who received the most nominations for possessing local influence. I talked to these men about their participation in local affairs and their views on the participation of other leaders.[2]

In February of 1967, I interviewed ethnic, religious, racial, and institutional spokesmen with regard to the support their respective groups accorded the mayor of the community before and after race riots occurred in the city (August, 1966). From these interviews, I learned a great deal about ethnic politics in the city.[3]

In the spring of 1967, I spent approximately ten days engaged in participant observation in the office of the mayor. These days were spread over a ten-week period but were selected to avoid bias as to day of the week. I was at no time asked to leave the office. I had access to all council and committee meetings and all conferences. I worked one day as the mayor's secretary and receptionist. At this time, I became interested in the office of the mayor and began systematically to clip articles in the local newspaper which mentioned activities of the mayor or the council. I continued to clip such articles for thirty months through August 1969.

During the summer of 1967, I engaged in an intensive study of two Waukegan issues selected for the high amount of controversy they produced in the city. These were urban renewal and school integration. Later I became interested in the controversy which developed around a proposed one-way street and investigated this issue also. With regard to these issues, I interviewed the persons and institutional representatives who had been involved in the controversies. I traced the issues through various public and private documents.[4] During the months I spent in this investigation, I continued sporadic observation in the office of the mayor.

The following summer, Mayor Sabonjian employed me as his private secretary, offering the job as a way I could "really learn a lot about the mayor's office." I spent three and one half months in this job, a participating member of the office staff as well as an observer of it. During these months of participant observation, I continued to have access to meetings and conferences, though complete attendance was restricted by the demands of my job. Other information became more available as a result of my participation. I had access to all communication going in and out of the office. I also had occasion to become better acquainted with other employees of the city and with the relations between the mayor's office and other departments. I terminated work in September of 1968 but continued throughout the winter and spring to be in close communication with the mayor. In June of 1969, I again worked as his secretary for a two-week period.

I did not tape record conversations or statements in the course of my study, but relied on daily reconstruction of events. Thus, quotations, although based on my notes, are printed as I recalled them. Statements which are accompanied by dates enclosed in parentheses are taken from the Waukegan *News-Sun* unless otherwise identified.

The focus of this research is the role of the mayor but the

analysis draws extensively on all of the data accumulated in these various projects. I believe the observations I was able to make of the mayor on a day-to-day basis provide my most important contribution.

In my analysis, I strenuously sought and included the deviant cases, that is, those events which ran contrary to my evolving theory. A full picture is thus presented.

My various research projects in Waukegan emerged over time, posing and responding to different questions. My first project, a rather mechanical study of reputational influence, turned up a strikingly small, seemingly cohesive and reputedly powerful elite. It consisted primarily of economic dominants in the community and was headed by the mayor, the newspaper publisher, and a local banker; these three were unanimous choices of thirty-nine respondents. My conclusions about this decision-making elite were shaken when nominated influentials sought out my list to learn who else had been named. More importantly, subsequent analyses of public issues failed to support this elitist model.

The issue analyses increased my interest in the mayor since respondents so often saw him as the crucial actor in deciding the kind of public issue I had now proposed to understand and to which my former model seemed inapplicable. Attribution of decision-making to the mayor appeared to be assumption as often as it was documented fact. But the felt presence of the mayor became increasingly noticeable.

Mayor Sabonjian was a highly controversial figure. After 1966 street violence, he gained national publicity for his blunt and flamboyant law and order program. Later, in 1970, he fired with impunity fifty-four members of his seventy-one man police force when they failed to report for duty and claimed illness. During his administration the city has tripled in size through annexation, and thus increased its economic advantage. The mayor is also proud of his recruiting raids on the industries of land-locked communities which can no longer provide the space and amenities sought by modern industries. Finally, he demonstrated he could win election in every precinct of his heterogeneous city.

Yet the mayor I observed in his office spent very little time resolving controversial disputes, organizing aggressive programs, taking directions or imposing his will. He did not fit into my conception of the chief executive—a man surrounded by advisors, proposals, budgets and ordinances. Nor did his day evoke the smoke-filled rooms of popular literature or the power plays of the headlines. Rather, I found behavior which bore greatest resemblance to a "Dear Abby" news column or a rough-and-ready hiring hall. The mayor spent ninety percent of his time with the homey personal problems of his constituents. Participant observation was eye-opening.

In the literature, I found little to help me organize my observations. Edward Banfield and Robert Dahl provided the only serious studies of local political executives. Both had abandoned the civics text approach to local government as uninformative; they sought to discover informal ways in which aggressive executives centralized power. Their analyses of controversial issues were suggestive of the nature and constraints of the mayoral role. In this book, I have relied heavily on their work.[5] There was little, however, which related to the predominant activities of a man who frequently found his way into controversial arenas yet seemed himself focused elsewhere.

Analyses of controversial issues limit investigation of the mayoral role to times of crises and bypass everyday situations. The implication is that the non-controversial is static or irrelevant.[6] It seems likely, however, that daily politics would be related to and consistent with headline politics. Indeed, this low level action is another whole aspect of the complete role of a political executive.

Another limitation of research based on the observation of controversy is the sporadic nature of such investigation. Analysis of a few moments in time either misses or assumes a web of underlying obligations, assumptions and behavior patterns which an organizational actor develops and manipulates. These continuing conditions are not visible on the surface, and yet they affect both the daily process of political influence and the exercise of headline influence.

Most importantly, my bafflement with early participant observation led me to a very open-ended curiosity as to what the mayor's job looked like to him; what were the constraints and coercions of the executive role; what was he up to . . . with such seeming success?

During my months of observation, I concluded that the mayor's activities could be organized in terms of his attempt to coordinate the symbiotic systems in the local area—to craft a political community. His municipality contained functional units and social groups which were differentiated and interdependent. Thus a kind of symbiotic cooperation occurred among units, but the potential for organization of differentiated groups into factions organized around opposing interests was naturally high.

The mayor took as his task the definition and satisfaction of complementary needs and the suppression or resolution of mutually contradictory demands for scarce resources. Because there is incomplete integration in the private and public organization of the community, potentially profitable exchanges may fail to occur: jobs may go unfilled in a city with suitable workers unemployed; programs may fail while potential support remains unknown. A coordinator who sees potential for mutually profitable cooperation, for multiple payoffs, may facilitate that cooperation without making the kind of choice which is associated with zero-sum politics (in which benefits to one party are necessarily losses to others). The benefits of unrealized cooperation increase the productivity of available resources; political power is created in the process.

Political heads infrequently feel such an ambitious responsibility to the political community. As Norton Long points out in "The Local Community as an Ecology of Games," there are few persons in any community who are apt to see "things in general" as their business. Government officials, the ones ostensibly charged with responsibility for the "whole," do not normally perceive themselves as "governors of the municipality" nor are they empowered to perform any such ambitious role. Rather, "the ideology of local government is a highly limited affair in which the office holders respond to demands and mediate conflicts." Further, Long notes, the possible development of significant government action has been blocked by separation of powers within the government and by separation of government from economics.[7]

While Sabonjian must deal with these limitations, he has an imposing image of his job. Believing firmly that it is better to work together than to work at cross-purposes and that it is the responsibility of the mayor to create the conditions of cooperation, Mayor Sabonjian has attacked in Waukegan the problem of political integration.

Chapter I of this book supplies background information on the city where the study was done and on the mayor who is the focus of attention.

Chapter II sets forth the group environment within which the mayor operates. The mayor's role is described in terms of his commitments to six population categories. He is constrained in his action by his responsibility to these groups which occupy different positions in the socio-economic structure of the community, control different resources, and make different demands upon the office of the mayor.

Chapter III is a description of the mayor's strategies for encouraging mutually beneficial cooperation among individuals, groups and institutions in the community. Acting as middle-man, he facilitates "horizontal integration"—cooperation among complementary interests in the community. Making himself useful in a broad range of situations where interests converge but appropriate links are missing, the mayor builds a strong base of popular support, an organization difficult to challenge, and a subtle but pervasive control.

The mayor seeks to avoid contradictions from arising among his commitments and to prevent disruption of his cooperative networks by maintaining multiple payoff rather than zero-sum definitions. It is to his advantage, therefore, to control the scale, timing, and definition of public issues. Means for exercising this control or, as Norton Long calls it, "setting the civic agenda," are discussed in Chapter IV.

Chapter V discusses the role of trust in facilitating cooperation in a system where cooperating units do not automatically trust either one another or the would-be organizer, the politician. Since trust is a vital precondition of political organization, its creation is an omnipresent aspect of the mayoral role. Three types of trust are discussed: trust in primary relation, trust in value representation and trust in role adequacy.

The final chapter is a summary, a statement of the general parameters underlying this analysis, and a comment on the mayor's world view.

NOTES

[1] Occupations and ethnic identifications of councilmen over the sixteen years between 1951 and 1967 were obtained from newspaper accounts, from knowledgeable people in the community and from interviews with the members of the 1965–1967 council. Data on other characteristics was secured only from the 1966 aldermen. This research is summarized in Ann Lennarson, "Power and Politics" (unpublished Honor's thesis, Lake Forest College, Lake Forest, Illinois, 1966). [Updated tabulations are recorded in "Power and Politics: A Community Analysis" (unpublished Master's paper, Northwestern University, Evanston, Illinois, 1967).]

[2] Lists of leaders were secured from five people selected for their knowledge of the pattern of local influence in various institutional sectors of city life. Raters included a public relations official, the editor of the newspaper, a lawyer active in local politics, a city government official, and a retail merchant from an old Waukegan family. They were asked to name the ten people they felt to be the most influential citizens in the city, not only in particular spheres of community endeavor but in a city-wide sense. It was made clear that the criterion for nomination was not to be civic spirit (although leaders might be civic minded), but local power. Nominees were to be persons who could get things done in the city or who could kill local projects. As individuals appeared on lists they were contacted and asked to submit similar lists. Each person who contributed names was asked to justify his choices. The final list, representing the composite of twenty-three private ratings — those of the original five consultants and of the top eighteen influentials — consisted of forty-nine names. Of these, fifteen received only one nomination and were therefore dropped from the list. The remaining thirty-four men were considered to be "top influentials." Lists were also obtained from each of the sixteen aldermen. Their ratings so closely paralleled the first list that it was possible to incorporate them without supplementing or changing any of the thirty-four names.

All statistics and discussion concerning influentials are based on data secured in private interviews with the top eighteen men from the list of thirty-four. These men received six or more nominations. *Ibid.*

[3] With regard to this project, the following persons were interviewed: Mayor Sabonjian, Democratic party chairman, Democratic party leader, Republican party chairman, ministers (West side, South side); president — NAACP, president — "Protector Rights" (black nationalist group), organizer "Protector Rights" (participant in riots), various riot participants; president — Puerto Rican Society, chairman — Mexican Festival Organization, president — Waukegan-Lake County Lithuanian Society, president — Slovenian National Paternal Organization (SNPT), officer — Finnish Historical Society, Greek Church leader.

[4] These two issues were urban renewal and school integration. Persons interviewed in connection with the urban renewal issue included: the mayor, the manager of the chamber of commerce, the 1966 president of the chamber of commerce, the president of the Downtown Council (at the time of the urban

renewal controversy), the chairman of the Greater Revitalization of Waukegan Committee (GROW), i.e. citizens' group for urban renewal, the librarian (member of the GROW committee and engineer of the successful library referendum), the president of the League of Women Voters, chairman of the League of Women Voters Committee on Housing and of the Urban Renewal Citizens' Workshop, and member of the Planning Commission during the 1950's, Democratic and Republican Party chairmen (county), Waukegan lawyer who was a member of the planning commission during all the years traced in this study and whose wife is a precinct committeewoman and former law partner of U.S. senator.

Persons interviewed in connection with the controversy over a one-way street included the mayor and other city officials, the manager of the chamber of commerce, downtown businessmen, and local youths.

Persons interviewed in connection with the school integration issue included: retired superintendent of schools who was the chief school executive during the years of the controversy, the plaintiff, school board members, the mayor, school principals and teachers. These findings are summarized in "Power and Politics: A Community Analysis" (unpublished Master's paper, Northwestern University, Evanston, Illinois 1967).

[5] Edward Banfield, *Political Influence* (Free Press, 1961); Robert Dahl, *Who Governs* (Yale University Press, 1961).

[6] Banfield, for example, states that: ". . . It is necessary to observe influence 'at work' rather than 'in repose.' Controversy seems to provide the best setting for such observation, for in controversy the contending actors not only exercise influence but do so more or less competitively . . . It must be hastily acknowledged, that the method . . . has its own peculiar limitations. For one thing, attention to controversy diverts attention from what is not 'actively' controversial (e.g. what is not in the headlines). That the Chicago Title and Trust Company levies a toll on every real estate transaction, that organized barbers charge the outrageous price of $2.00 for a haircut, that newspaper delivery trucks travel 70 miles an hour on streets closed to commercial traffic — these are all evidences of influence at work. But in these matters the influence relationship, having been established some time ago and having not been called into question recently, lies outside the ken of the researcher who associates influence with controversy. In such 'steady state' situations nothing 'happens' and therefore case studies cannot be written." *Political Influence*, p. 9.

[7] Norton Long, "The Local Community As An Ecology of Games," *American Journal of Sociology* 64 (November, 1958): 255.

1

Background

THE COMMUNITY

Waukegan, Illinois is located on the west shore of Lake Michigan, thirty-five miles north of Chicago and fifty miles south of Milwaukee.[1] Waukegan's history goes back to 1788 when a fort was established on the site. Permanent settlers came to "Little Fort" in 1835 and in 1843 the growing community became the County Seat of Lake County. It was incorporated as a village in 1859.

According to the 1970 census of the population, 64,665 persons resided in Waukegan. In 1960, the figure was 55,719. The 1960 federal census is the only source available for many of the statistics I will report here although I have used more recent data whenever it was available.

Contiguous with Waukegan's southern boundary is the satellite community of North Chicago. It is the site of several major industrial complexes and of the huge Great Lakes Naval Training Center. Forty-three percent of all the United States Navy recruits are trained at this base, some eighty thousand in 1968.[2] Two-thirds of North Chicago's population (47,275 in 1970) is military. Waukegan and the non-base portion of North Chicago have historically behaved much as a single unit. North Chicago industries are some of Waukegan's largest employers. Among these is Abbott Laboratories, the area's largest employer. Until 1954, when a high school was built in North Chicago, the youths of the two communities attended a common institution in Waukegan. On the western fringes of Waukegan are two tiny municipalities. With fewer than three thousand residents, Gurnee is an undifferentiated extension of Waukegan. Park City is a trailer camp owned by a single man who is also its mayor.

While a disproportionate share of the area's lower income and black residents reside in North Chicago, the norm for the city of Waukegan remains heterogeneity. With the partial exception of North Chicago, suburbs do not absorb homogeneous elements of

9

the population. The city is diversified with regard to age, occupation, religion, income and ethnicity. All occupational categories used in census classifications are represented in substantial numbers. Over fifty churches are located in the city as well as a wide variety of ethnic groups. In 1960, the census reported that 14,784 of Waukegan's 55,719 residents claimed foreign extraction. Twenty-seven different countries were represented. Of these, the most important in terms of size, solidarity, and formal organization are the Finns, the Lithuanians, and the Slovenians.

The Puerto Ricans are not listed among the foreign-born population but reliable estimates in 1968 suggested that there were six thousand Puerto Ricans living in Waukegan. This group is tightly organized into the Puerto Rican Society. Moreover, it is allied with a Mexican population (approximately three thousand) into a Spanish-speaking block.[3] According to area politicians, this block can still produce a directed vote. It is therefore the most important voting block in the city.

In 1960, the black population in Waukegan was about 8.5 percent of the population. In 1970, it was 13 percent. Of Waukegan's two black neighborhoods, the larger and less prosperous adjoins a black concentration in North Chicago. In that city, the civilian population is 23 percent black.[4] Thus, during the years of this study, there were between ten and fifteen thousand blacks in the border area of the two cities. While important in numbers and spatially concentrated in two neighborhoods, the blacks in Waukegan lack solidarity and organization. In 1966 and again in 1967, I attempted to interview black leaders but was unable to locate any whose leadership was generally acknowledged. Black spokesmen agreed that overall organization was lacking and that existing groups were conflicted.

Ethnic groups are less spatially segregated than in earlier times, but there are distinct patterns. Generally speaking, an east-west street is assumed to divide ethnic Waukegan from non-ethnic Waukegan. Within the south side ethnic area, blacks are aggregated nearest the lake (east) in the oldest housing. One goes west into Puerto Rican and Mexican neighborhoods, on into Finnish areas and finally into the Lithuanian and Slovenian neighborhoods which are the newer areas. Other ethnic enclaves are scattered among these.

Traditionally, the street which separated ethnics from non-ethnics also represented a voting line. South of Washington Street the vote was Democratic, north of Washington Street it was Republican. The north side usually won. The election of the man who preceded the present mayor (now acting majority leader in the Illinois Senate) recalls a common pattern. Precincts were numbered north to south in such a way as to give all the low numbers to south side precincts and the high numbers to those on the north side. The election in 1952 showed the winning candidate to have lost *all* of the first eleven precincts and to have won *all* of the remaining precincts (seventeen) for 55 percent of the total vote.

While the population of the city has a large industrial work force (in 1960, 36 percent of the labor force was engaged in manufacturing), and a high ethnic percentage, it is by no means a poor community. The city's industries are prosperous and pay well. In 1966 estimates of median income per household put Waukegan at $9,437. The diversification of these industries has been an important factor in the relative stability of the city's economy and the stability of its incomes. One hundred and thirty manufacturing establishments producing over 450 different products are located in the Waukegan-North Chicago urban area. The six largest employers in 1969 were Abbott Laboratories with 5400 employees (pharmaceuticals and chemicals), Outboard Marine with 5200 (outboard motors), Fansteel Metalurgical Corporation with 3200 (automotive and high speed tools), Johns-Manville Corporation with 2000 (asbestos products), U.S. Steel with 1400, and Warwick Electronics with 1100.

There is good reason to believe that job opportunities were abundant during the years of this study. A newspaper editorial in 1967 emphasized the increase in job opportunities which had accompanied the wide industrial expansion of the preceding decade (8-26-67). The Waukegan office of the Illinois Employment Service reported in 1967 that unemployment for the area was eight-tenths of one percent. A newspaper survey examining opportunities for Negroes (1967) reported an over-abundance of jobs. This reaffirmed statements made by industrialists distressed by the worker shortage, and the reports of businessmen regarding the failure of programs designed to recruit black workers. Half of the skilled and semi-skilled black workers interviewed in the newspaper survey were dissatisfied with their promotion record (half were not) but none reported an inability to find employment. A sample survey taken in 1966 by Robert Bell of Northern Illinois University indicated that in the Waukegan census tract with the highest percentage of blacks, only twenty to twenty-five percent stated they would prefer to change jobs (11-1-66). Of the 500 workers newly employed in the county between March and May of 1968, 450 were women (7-23-68).

In 1960, home ownership was 57 percent for the city as a whole; black home ownership was 43 percent. The census tract with the highest percentage of black residents (lowest income, lowest home ownership) showed 22 percent of the units to have more than one person per room.

Contributing to Waukegan's prosperity is its position as the retail center of Lake County which in 1961 ranked seventy-seventh in the nation in retail sales per household. In 1966 the county ranked sixth in the nation in per family income. Retail sales amount to two hundred million dollars annually, 80 percent of which occur in Waukegan. The payoff to the city government is enormous in many ways—income to residents, sales and property taxes. The sales tax revenue alone (which is used at city discretion) contributed one million dollars to the budget in 1968.[5]

As an industrial, retail, and population center, Waukegan dominates the county. Moreover, important industries in the area are home-owned or home-based. The corporate headquarters of the three largest employers, Abbott Laboratories, Outboard Marine, and Fansteel, are in the area. While the corporate headquarters of Johns-Manville is elsewhere, at least two top level officials advanced from the Waukegan plant. Thus, while Waukegan is near both Chicago and Milwaukee, its economic base is primarily local. Paralleling this locally centered economy are locally contained and focused political institutions.

The government structure in Waukegan is mayor-aldermanic with a full-time mayor.[6] Mayor and aldermen are elected by the city in partisan elections. The mayor, who is elected by the city at large, serves a four-year term as chief executive. Eight wards elect sixteen aldermen (two aldermen per ward) to serve four-year terms on the city council. Half are elected in alternate two-year periods.

Illinois law grants to the City of Waukegan the responsibility for health, safety and public welfare. This includes responsibility for regulation of land use through zoning; regulation of building construction, and maintenance of streets and sidewalks; health regulations; water and sewer supply.

Illinois statute further designates the means by which government finances shall be procured. City revenue is collected through taxes on real estate, personal property, fees and permits, licenses, court and traffic fines, wheel taxes, parking receipts, the motor fuel tax, sewer and water charges, and the city's share of the sales tax. The city clerk controls the general tax fund and is empowered to transfer or loan money from one fund to another. In providing city services Waukegan has relied on general revenue rather than special assessments. The total city budget for the fiscal year ending April 1968 was $7,016,437.

The mayor, as the city's chief executive, is charged with city administration. He appoints a great many city officials, city boards and city committees.[7] Such officials as the police chief, the superintendent of streets, the building commissioner, the superintendent of sewer and water facilities, and the various building inspectors are appointed by and directly responsible to the mayor. The mayor has no administrative assistant and there is no deputy mayor.

With respect to the council, the mayor's position is potentially strong. In addition to appointing city officials, he appoints council committees and reserves a veto power; a two-thirds council majority is required to override him.

Thus the mayor's power is lodged in three areas of interest which he controls directly or indirectly through control of the council. These are: (1) legality: licensing, permits and regulations—e.g., liquor licensing, zoning, building, law enforcement; (2) the economic benefits of city government as an ongoing enterprise—e.g., jobs and corporate purchasing; (3) the distribution of governmentally supplied goods and services—e.g., street service, utility extensions, garbage collection.

Waukegan has traditionally elected Republicans. Since 1951, there have been forty-seven Republican aldermen and only twenty-one Democrats. Nevertheless, non-partisan and cross-party campaigning are common. In 1965, 63 percent of the local ballots were split. In recent years, aldermanic posts have been dominated by manual laborers, sales and clerical workers and proprietors of small business enterprises. They have represented an array of ethnic groups, except blacks and women (who have only since

1969 begun to enter politics as candidates). The typical alderman's schooling equals the median for his age group; he is a native mid-westerner and a long-term resident of the city. No alderman was named as a community influential when a list of such persons was compiled (in spite of the fact that all 1966 aldermen were interviewed in this survey).[8]

Persons nominated as locally influential came overwhelmingly from the business world. All were professionals, self-employed businessmen, managers or high level officials. Except for judges, the mayor was the only political official mentioned. He was also the only non-Jewish ethnic. Other influentials tended to be Old American types, descended from Western European settlers. Typically they, too, are Protestant, are native mid-westerners and most often home-town boys. Among the younger men, the chances are good that they are highly educated.[9]

THE MAYOR

In 1957, Robert Sabonjian was the unlikely victor of the Waukegan mayoral elections. Sabonjian, the son of Armenian immigrants, was a Democrat and a south sider. Only two of the thirty-three mayors who had preceded him in office had been Democrats and south side mayors were unknown.

Sabonjian had since 1951 been the alderman of the second ward, a highly ethnic area with a preponderance of blacks. His daughter was the only white child in her class. Sabonjian was the proprietor of a small dry cleaning establishment and had served also as postmaster.

Sabonjian's democratic nomination for mayor seems to have gone unnoticed by the newspaper. In the weeks preceding the 1957 election, his name and the news of his campaign are conspicuously absent.

Yet, when the election was over, he had won the mayoralty. The Chicago *Daily News* (4-18-57) reported:

WAUKEGAN'S NEW MAYOR FOE OF ALL—EXCEPT VOTERS: GOP, DEM BOSSES STILL BLINKING AT SABONJIAN'S ELECTION UPSET

Waukegan's top politicians, still blinking at Tuesday's election results, are asking: "How did Bob Sabonjian get elected mayor?"

The "Little Armenian" had no platform and no headquarters except a street corner, ran against the Republicans, denounced the Democrats, criticized veterans' clubs, blasted gamblers, insulted minority groups and was refused help by his running mates.

"Everyone else voted for me," he says.

Sabonjian, 41, spent $800 on his campaign—much of it for handbills he passed out on corners.

He whipped a smooth running Republican organization that spent many times that amount to beat him.

At times it was hard to figure who he was running against. He just as frequently roasted Chicago's Mayor Daley as he did his Republican opponent, Harry Kilbane.

Sabonjian is a short man with swarthy features.

Folks call him "The Rock" because he fancies himself the Gibraltar of Waukegan's South Side.

When someone said his appearance would be against him in the election, he slapped pictures of himself on auto roofs and in store windows.

The Rock's logic is phenomenal.

When he opened a cleaning shop in Waukegan he named it the Dutch Mill, "to get up high in the phone book."

"But, why not call it the Armenian Mill and get higher?" he was asked.

"What!" he snorted. "And lose the Turkish trade?"

Sabonjian started out as a caddy at Skokie Country Club in Glencoe. He was later a bell-hop at Northmoor Country Club, Highland Park, and a $7-a-week service station attendant.

His political career started in 1951 when he was elected alderman from the 2nd ward.

He quit to become acting postmaster, a job he lost when the GOP took over Washington. He was re-elected alderman two years ago.

A true fighter, he once exchanged blows on the city hall steps with a fellow Democratic alderman.

When Sabonjian decided to put his name on the ballot in the mayoral primary, he borrowed a pass key to sneak into city hall at 4 A.M. and beat two regular Democrat candidates in line.

"I'll win five to one," he said—and he did.

"It's just a question of time before I take over," he announced in the Republican city hall on election night.

He did that, too, 8,518 to 6,799. Returns showed that 2500 Republicans split their ballots in his favor Tuesday.

When he "takes over" May 6, he'll have one Democratic alderman on his side.

"I don't expect any trouble. I'm for the people," he says.

A couple of circumstances, one coincidental and one calculated, seem to have contributed to this upset. Coincidentally, there had been considerable conflict within the Republican party over the nomination of its candidate. Not all of this conflict had been resolved by the final election. In addition, Sabonjian had some unlikely Republican support. The would-be mayor had worked hard in south side precincts for school board candidates favored by prominent north side citizens, and he had produced results. As one observer said: "Sabonjian taught the north side how to get out the south side vote." These citizens now returned that favor.

Once in office, Sabonjian lost no time in consolidating his power. His subsequent elections can not be connected with coincidence. His popularity in terms of both total votes and distribution of votes rose steadily through the 1965 election. When, in that year, he sought an unprecedented third term, he won in every precinct in the city, with 65 percent of the total city vote. The city clerk and city treasurer elected to serve with him were Republicans. A majority of the ballots were split. Table I summarizes Sabonjian's electoral history through 1965.

TABLE I

RESULTS OF WAUKEGAN MAYORAL ELECTIONS,
1957–1965*

| | NUMBER OF PRECINCTS FOR: | | | PERCENTAGES OF POPULAR VOTE |
YEAR	SABONJIAN	OPPONENT	TIED	FOR SABONJIAN
1957	18	14	0	55
1961	38	1	1	59
1965	46	0	0	65

*City of Waukegan, Illinois. Canvas of the Vote, 1957, 1961, 1965.

In the summer of 1966, violence broke out in Waukegan and Sabonjian's law and order reaction brought him national publicity. Although the actual destruction was minor and confined to a four-block stretch of road, Sabonjian's extreme reaction was newsworthy. He cut short his California vacation to return to the city and personally halt the disturbances. Calling the rioters "winos" and "scum," Sabonjian cordoned off the area, jailed record numbers of persons (under charges as severe as "treason"), called in the state troopers and the police forces of neighboring towns, took steps to halt the welfare payments of the trouble-makers, and pushed through (in the midst of the tumult) a city bill requiring that each participant in a public demonstration obtain beforehand a permit to participate (the acquisition of which depended upon absence of a police record). If, Sabonjian held, people want to be treated like first-class citizens and not animals, they should behave like first-class citizens and not animals.

Waukeganites were accustomed to Sabonjian's explosive personality. Earlier in the summer, for example, he had responded with similar language, vicious accusations and promises of posse capture when white residents had burned a cross in the yard of a black family moving into a white neighborhood. The press, however, picked up only the second incident. In response to their reporting, a deluge of mail arrived in Sabonjian's office (fifteen hundred letters within a month). Letters applauded the actions of the "law and order" mayor (the stand was not yet popular among politicians) and urged him to run for higher office. Accepting substantial and organized offers of financial backing, Sabonjian began a whirlwind campaign as an independent write-in candidate for the United States Senate. He ran against two of the most popular politicians in Illinois, Paul Douglas and Charles Percy. His law and order platform collected a tiny percentage of the total state vote.

In Lake County, however, seven thousand persons wrote in Sabonjian as their candidate for the senate. Ninety percent of these were in Waukegan proper. Observers in the area did not feel, however, that these votes could be attributed to the law and order campaign. When interviewed, ethnic leaders agreed that the riots were unimportant in the attachment of their people to the mayor. The riots did not occur in their neighborhood (thereby were unimportant generally), or "We grew up with Bobby; my people are loyal to him" (issue of riots unimportant), or "Oh, Bobby talks like that." The last remark was made by several black spokesmen.

The Democratic party chairman, although personally opposed to Sabonjian's "one man show," stated that he thought the effect of the riots would be negligible. He thought some opposition groups (especially NAACP) would attempt to use the issue to defeat Sabonjian in a couple of precincts but that the majority of blacks and whites would return the mayor to office. The mayor's personal machine, the party chairman said, was the strongest political force in the county. Issues, in comparison, were always unimportant.

The Republican party chairman seconded these views. Noting the large number of senate votes which Sabonjian got in the area, he said the mayor would continue to win by large margins. The backlash vote he thought would be trivial as would be the black reaction. "Sabonjian will win with city wide support. The riots had little impact on the average citizen. And he'll win no matter what ticket he runs on. He doesn't need party support."

The 1969 election results suggested that the views of these men were correct. A well-financed campaign, supported by important state officials (including the state treasurer, Adlai Stevenson III) was leveled against Sabonjian. Although the public emphasis of the opposition campaign was on good government, it was conceived by its organizing liberals around the need for bettering race relations in the community through a more liberal administration. The mayor lost in six of the city's fifty-three precincts where about a third of the vote went to him. These areas were predominantly black. Just what these precinct votes mean is unclear since there is no data available to indicate specific black/non-black voting in precincts which are not homogeneous. No one thought the blacks abandoned Sabonjian on a large scale, although their residential areas were canvassed heavily by opposition workers.

Opposition workers were disappointed in the black vote as well as the three to one defeat of their candidate in the city as a whole. In explanation, an opposition worker told the *Chicago Daily News* (4-16-69):

> "Sabonjian has been able to keep a lid on the black community, and the white community likes this. The only precincts where we got a plurality were the black areas, and we didn't do as well there as we expected."

Another backer, himself black, told this paper that the blacks didn't turn out against Sabonjian because they were "scared."

A confounding factor in analyzing these election results, however, is Sabonjian's change in the 1969 election from the Democratic to the Republican label. Prior to the 1969 vote Sabonjian speculated on the results of this change. Referring to his ethnic supporters generally, he remarked that many would vote for him and the others would stay home.

"Some of the people won't want to vote Republican," he said, "but if they don't know the Democratic candidate, they'll most likely stay home." It seems probable that many of the persons who would have the greatest difficulty in dealing with a party-personality dilemma would be black, and that there would be a high stay-at-home percentage among them for this reason.

Analysis of the voting figures in precincts where Sabonjian lost, suggests that party shift may explain the losses better than the race issue. Table II shows the vote totals in these precincts for 1965 when Sabonjian was the Democratic candidate and for 1969 when Sabonjian was the Republican candidate.

TABLE II

MAYORAL ELECTION, 1965 & 1969:
COMPARISON OF PARTY VOTE IN SIX BLACK PRECINCTS
LOST BY SABONJIAN IN 1969*

| | VOTES: | | | | | |
| PRECINCT | REPUBLICAN | | DEMOCRATIC | | TOTAL VOTE | |
	1965	1969	1965	1969	1965	1969
A	82	134	449	258	531	392
B	37	94	255	213	292	307
C	29	16	189	159	218	175
D	65	65	265	118	330	183
E	53	96	157	113	210	209
F	89	145	368	310	457	455
	355	550	1683	1171	2038	1721

*City of Waukegan, Illinois. Canvas of the Vote, 1965, 1969.

These figures show that total voter turnout in these precincts dropped 16 percent (317 votes) when Sabonjian switched party. The Republican vote increased by 55 percent (195 votes); the Democratic vote decreased by 30 percent (512 votes). In these old and built-up neighborhoods, it is unlikely that population increase accounted for the Republican gains. It appears that the

512-vote Democratic loss is explained by the 195 vote Republican gain and the 317 stay-at-home Democrats.

The same trend is apparent in the Democratic precincts which Sabonjian carried as a Republican. His overall percentages dropped throughout the ethnic precincts but enough voters switched party to allow his Republican victory. It is possible that the race issue kept the black precincts from *going* Republican as did the majority of formerly Democratic precincts (although the vote changes were in the same direction).

Two additional factors may explain the degree of switchover. One is the original degree of commitment to the Democratic party which I suggested earlier may be greatest among lower-class black voters. Middle-class blacks (precincts E and F) were more apt to switch party than lower-class blacks in whose precincts the turnout dropped.

The second factor involves the effects of an unusual campaign move on the part of Sabonjian. When he declared his new party affiliation, the mayor stated that he was still loyal to his Democratic supporters and urged them to write his name in on their primary ballots. His political subleaders canvassed the ethnic strongholds to urge voters to participate in the write-in of Sabonjian for the Democratic nomination. The results were amazing. The declared Democratic candidate received 1289 votes in the primary; Sabonjian received 881 write-in votes (40 percent of the total). These votes are unfortunately not identified by precincts. It is possible that the mayor's switch-over campaign was handled more efficiently in some precincts than in others, or that in the target areas (black precincts) of the opposition campaign the mayor's plea was confused by canvassers from his opposition. The results of the switch-over campaign in the primary may have had important effects on the final election returns in various precincts. At any rate, the final returns of the 1969 election showed that in the city as a whole, Sabonjian had won his largest victory, collecting 74 percent of the total vote.

Large campaign victories are matched by exclamations as to the mayor's effectiveness in achieving goals. A former member of Mayor Daley's legal staff who has real estate dealings in Waukegan, stated unequivocally that Mayor Sabonjian was stronger in his city than Mayor Daley was in Chicago. The sixteen aldermen on the Waukegan City Council in 1966 asserted that the council invariably rubber-stamped the proposals of the mayor. A special in the Waukegan *News-Sun* (9-26-68) entitled "The Waukegan City Council in Action" reported that:

> . . . what gets passed is what the city's 16 aldermen can agree on. Ordinarily they are very agreeable, especially to each other and to Mayor Robert Sabonjian.
>
> The mayor presides at council sessions, which he operates as he once said, "according to Robert's Rules of Order—and my first name is Robert."
>
> As one alderman said: "You almost don't have to have a council. All he (the mayor) needs us for is to make it legal. . ."
>
> Apparently the public appreciates a strong mayor. Election after election voters show their confidence in the way he runs the city by swamping anyone who runs against him.

The corporation counsel who watches the intricacies of city legislation said in 1966: "We have a one man government named Robert Sabonjian." He continued:

> Sabonjian is a real curiosity. He's inclusive. He not only brings together groups that don't logically belong together but he gets consulted on things he has nothing to do with. . . .

The woman who was secretary to Coulson (the mayor who preceded Sabonjian) and who is presently secretary to Sabonjian said:

> Coulson was much more legalistic than Sabonjian. . . . So with him, things took much longer or never occurred at all. Bob steps on toes, of course, doing things the way he does, but he gets things done. Coulson was very tuned in to the notion of give and take; Sabonjian is much more given to central direction. The people end up appreciating it. He's much more popular than Coulson was.

Another city hall observer said of the two mayors:

> Coulson spoke a different language from the people or the council. He seemed to alienate the aldermen by talking so far beyond them. He couldn't sell himself because he didn't have a warm enough personality. Bobby can sell anything.

In 1969, the local newspaper urged the mayor's reelection:

> Waukegan's Mayor Robert Sabonjian, seeking his fourth term in office has proved himself over and over as a forceful, conscientious and effective administrator. He has almost singlehandedly forged

a progressive and cooperative spirit in Waukegan, a city hobbled for years by disunity and lack of purpose (4-11-69).

All ethnic leaders interviewed in this study, with the exception of a few black spokesmen, responded in effect: "Bobby is good for my people."

The only union leader who is reputed to have any influence in the local community, asserted that "Bobby is the best mayor Waukegan has ever had."

The "Rock," as Sabonjian is now known throughout Waukegan, arrived at this position of enormous, unrefuted, and largely approved power through a certain kind of political style. "I bring a peculiar form of honesty to public office and I do a job," he said. Others clearly agree he is effective and his "straight-talking" has given him national publicity. His campaign letters in 1969 (his only campaign technique that year) stated these emphases in tone and in content.

Dear Friend:

Once again I am asking you for your support and help. I ask you to be sure and vote this Tuesday, April 15th. I need your help in winning this election . . . .

This week you will hear a lot of political slogans and promises to do a better job than I have. I am sure you know that in my own way I have done as much as I could humanly do to make you feel that Waukegan is in good hands and will continue to be a great city with your help.

The letters did not ring of the centralized power and "efficient administration" portrayed by the press and the community's influentials. They evoked rather the descriptions of the mayor's job given by city employees. The woman who was secretary to the mayor in 1967 described the job in this way:

Well, he plays priest—counsels people with their family problems and their money problems and things like that. He helps out girls who have got pregnant and he finds people jobs. He signs bills, presides over council meetings, campaigns to get the candidates he wants elected. He helps organizations, like the Downtown Waukegan Council, straighten out their problems when they get in a stalemate or something. He intervenes between them and the other side to reach a compromise or help them get what they want some other way. And he works to get industries here and keep them happy. . . . He helps them get the zoning they need or straighten out their labor problems. He'll mediate between labor and management when a union is on strike and things like that. Sometimes bringing in other kinds of industry will be helpful to them or maybe its a matter of keeping competitors out.

"How," she was asked in this interview, "does he manage to do these things?" She replied: "Because he's such a marvelous persuader, I guess. That's why he's such a strong mayor." Pressed on these statements, she stated that she felt that the reason Sabonjian was so strong was:

Mostly, I think, because he wants to be. He's very proud that *anybody* will come to him with their problems, and that he will help them, so . . . This is my theory. It starts much smaller than this but the word gets around: "Go see the mayor; he'll help you. . . ." It goes back to the vote system. If you're going to get a lot of votes you've got to have a lot of people behind you. By helping virtually everybody in the town, Sabonjian gets everyone behind him.

With this, we are back where we started. Here is a man, a servant of the people, who close observers say spends most of his time helping others. One suspects there is power underlying this ability to help so many, so often. And indeed, one is told that this mayor has very great power, that he is a one man government given to centralized, if not dictatorial direction.

The mayor, as his letter indicates, believes both stories—that he is the servant of the people and the man in charge.

NOTES

[1] Waukegan-North Chicago Chamber of Commerce, *Industrial and Economic Survey of Waukegan-North Chicago-Gurnee, Illinois* (March 1, 1967).

[2] Lake County Board of Supervisors, *County of Lake* (1968), p. 40.

[3] Estimates of the Presidents of the Puerto Rican Society and the Mexican Festival Organization.

[4] Twenty-three percent nonwhite is the 1960 figure for North Chicago. In 1970, the population at Great Lakes Naval Training Center were enumerated as part of North Chicago. The percentage black in this more inclusive unit was only 17 percent but the decrease is probably due to the inclusion of the base in the count.

[5] The city sales tax revenue for the past few years has been: Year ending

April, 1968: $941,440; 1969: $1301,000; 1970: $1455,006; 1971: $1898,-900.

[6] The law provides for fourteen aldermen to represent the first thirty thousand citizens with two additional aldermen to be elected for each additional twenty thousand.

[7] Subject to the consent of the council, the mayor appoints the following city officials: corporation counsel, city prosecutor, police chief, city engineer, superintendent of streets, fire chief, city physician, health inspector, superintendent of water works, business manager of water works, city collector and purchasing agent, building commissioner, city electrician, heating and air-conditioning inspector, electrical inspector, plumbing inspector, housing inspector, playground and recreation director, city chaplain, director of planning, harbor master, parking meter collector.

He also appoints the board of local improvements, the parking commission, the grade school board (until 1970), the civil service board, the housing authority, the labor relations board, library board, municipal band committee, planning commission, playgrounds and recreation board, zoning board of appeals, civil board of decency, the commission on human relations, one member of the hospital board and two members of the port authority.

Ruth Gregory, ed., *Its Past, Its Present* (League of Women Voters and the City of Waukegan, 1967), p. 19.

[8] See Lennarson, *supra,* Introduction, note 1.

[9] See Lennarson, *supra,* Introduction, note 2.

2

The Mayor's Cage
of Pressures

In a politico-economic system where resources of action are dispersed and controlled by diverse and potentially conflicting interests, a political actor can pursue a course of action only within a strategy which incorporates and responds to the independent strategies of the various parties. Edward Banfield and Robert Dahl have described the aggressive political head as an entrepreneur who, aware of the limitations of his formal power, manipulates the resources at his disposal in such a way as to increase his access to resources, thereby increasing his power.

If, they argue, popularity (or money or status or whatever) can be used to achieve office, the resources of office, such as legality, patronage, and city contracts, can then be used to acquire further resources. Insofar as the owners of these resources are willing to swap with the elected official, the political head can centralize control. Some persons will be willing to trade political resources, such as their vote, for petty favors such as jobs and contracts. Others will swap their resources, such as campaign contributions, for larger favors such as preferential zoning. Even the most autonomous community figures will swap resources, such as control over the media, for "legality," defined as "conformity with the law, as the law is prescribed, interpreted, and enforced by government officials." A politician who centralizes power through drawing out and combining resources reduces what Dahl calls "slack" in the system of influences, i.e., unused or inefficiently used resources of power.[1]

Since he must trade, however, a political head does not centralize influence at trivial cost or on a permanent basis. As Banfield says:

> Those who sell him their bits of influence demand something in return: jobs, party preferment, or 'other bits of influence.' Thus some of the influence he has centralized he must again decentralize

by trading it for other bits that he particularly needs. He may have a sizeable 'inventory' and many 'accounts receivable' but if his 'accounts payable' are large, his net position is not good.[2]

In studying the effect of group claims on executive decision, researchers have looked at community controversies where competing claims seemed clearly focused. The structural position of a political head caught among multiple demands is inadequately described in these studies, although the study of controversial issues allowed Banfield and Dahl to formulate useful models of executive roles.

Scott Greer has proposed a model which does not restrict attention to the visible and dramatic aspects of political activity. In his discussion of the role of labor leaders, he suggests that successful union governance requires attention to two types of relationships which exert pressure on the leader and limit his options. Dynamic relations, those demanding action or resolution, are "problems." Equally important are relationships which have been stabilized (however temporarily). These he calls "commitments."[3] This twofold focus is important since a stabilized relationship is always a potential problem. It may become problematic in response to a development outside the system which changes the balance among commitments or through contradictions among the claims of the politician's various commitments. Greer says of the local labor leaders he studied:

> It is the number of forces and the inherent conflicts between them which cause labor leaders to work continually at stabilizing vital relationships. The general strategy is not to abolish opposing pressures (this is usually impossible) but rather to seek accommodation. Agreement reduces the objective insecurity for each party, and at the same time commits each party. It narrows the range of alternatives and increases predictability. However, in stabilizing these pressures the leader commits himself to specific behavior. . . . The more necessary such commitments are for the leader's security and the local's strength, the less likely their violation.[4]

Thus Greer looks at the labor leader's "cage of pressures"—the aggregate of relationships he must keep in balance. These include his responsibility to the international, to the union members, to other labor leaders, and to management and the contract. The goal is to specify the alternatives available to a leader with a given set of commitments.

The political head is similarly limited by his need to maintain an adequate or favorable balance of trade with the various persons and groups which possess control over resources important to his security and ability to act. The purpose here is to specify the commitments of a political head in a system of dispersed resources. The extent of controversy was not a criterion for the selection of instances used in this chapter; these are taken from observations of the daily activities of the mayor and the newspaper coverage of his ongoing activities.

Attending to this bulk data, the role of the political head may be described in terms of his commitments to six population categories. These categories are derived from crossing two variables: political autonomy and political participation.

Political Autonomy

	Low	Medium	High
Systematic (Actors)	A Subleaders	B Interest Advocates	C Institutional Dominants
Non-systematic (Constituents)	D Following	E Good Government Voters	F Indifferent Upper Class

Participation

Autonomy exists in control over resources of power, in alternative courses of action, in choice. It results in increased self-confidence, however misplaced. Socio-economic advantages are the most common factors which yield such choice, but overtime commitment to a position or relationship may be important in limiting alternatives. Coming into play are all of the resources Dahl identified as politically important: 1) money and credit, 2) jobs, 3) information, 4) social standing, 5) knowledge and expertness, 6) popularity, esteem, charisma, 7) legality, constitutionality, 8) ethnic solidarity, 9) the right to vote.[5]

Participation in the political process is seen as systematic or non-systematic. *Political actors* are those persons who are repetitively involved in political action. They are assumed to be reasonably knowledgeable about the processes and channels of political action and to have established the relationships, alliances, and communications which are necessary to the attainment of goals through this kind of action. *Constituents* are considered to be the bulk of persons in the general public who may vote in elections, but who do not, except as individual "clients," normally engage in attempts to influence government decisions.

Systematic participants in terms of increasing autonomy are subleaders, pressure groups, and community leaders. Unsystematic participants include the "following," the "good government" voters, and an indifferent upper class. The mayor is committed to groups which occupy different positions in the socio-economic structure of the community, wield different types of power, make different types of demands, and experience different levels of awareness. These groups constitute his "cage of pressures." His responsibility to them limits his alternatives. The following discussion will explore the nature of the commitment and the nature of the problems which accompany it. Also worthy of consideration is the relative importance of the various commitments for the mayor's security in office and action potential. The preceding chart will be used as a reference point.

POLITICAL ACTORS

Subleaders Low autonomy participants are, in this model, the political subleaders. They achieve claim to office, power, or other gain through unqualified support of a political leader, in this case the mayor. In the literature this relationship is usually discussed with regard to subleaders who are party lieutenants. In Sabonjian's Waukegan, subleaders are a cadre of non-party, but nonetheless loyal and trusted persons who can be counted on to support unconditionally the mayor's positions and programs. The group consists of various city officials appointed by the Mayor or elected because of him, aldermen, city employees, a scattered collection of informants, campaign workers, and others.

While the mayor may have to negotiate hard deals elsewhere to see programs realized, subleaders are solid supporters. The events which surrounded two favored mayoral programs are illustrative. Debates raged between the mayor and county officials, state officials, officials of other communities, developers, and property owners over the final jurisdiction which would incorporate the one hundred million dollar Lakehurst Shopping Mall. Unanimously supporting the mayor's negotiations, the Waukegan City Council took the steps which were necessary to end the debate and bring the mall into Waukegan. The shopping center was captured for Waukegan as a result of the city's demonstrating its singular ability to supply the proposed site with needed roads, water and sewer facilities. Under Sabonjian's leadership, the council handily approved the necessary expansion programs, conditionally committing up to 5.5 million dollars in expenditures. It approved a proposal which allowed Park City, a land-locked community through which a corridor was needed if Waukegan were to annex the property, to receive water from the Waukegan lines—as an incentive to approve the corridor. It took minor actions such as allowing property owners to petition for annexation to Waukegan. Throughout the battle, the council acted to strengthen the mayor's hand.

The council behaved similarly with regard to the mayor's plans for a civic center. When the mayor became interested in the project, the council approved without delay a six thousand dollar feasibility study. It stood behind him in his negotiations with the park board for the donation of a park where the mayor hoped to locate the civic center. It confirmed his reminders of the many properties the city had donated to the park district, as well as his reiteration that the city intended to continue this policy. And it continued to approve donations from the city to the park district. When the park board set up conditions which it said the city had to meet if the donation were to occur, the council approved them.

Other subleaders were also active. An alderman who was a member of the park board fought hard. He resisted a personal attack from the chairman of the board who accused him of a conflict of interest. Stating that he had never seen the mayor so excited about a project before, the alderman challenged the board president with "Don't you have confidence in the mayor?" and "Sabonjian's no fool."

Later, a wider group became involved. The board, with two members resisting the grant, set a public hearing to consider the proposal. The *News-Sun* grossly underestimated the situation in its report that:

An overflow crowd, heavily *sprinkled* with city employees, jammed the Waukegan Park Board office Tuesday night and overwhelmingly favored a plan which would transfer nine acres of Wahington Park to the city for a civic center site. (8-21-68)—[Emphasis added.]

The article quoted specifically the supportive remarks of the mayor's secretary and the city collector.

Although the maintenance of this structure of reliable support is an order of major importance to the mayor, and perhaps his second most time-consuming activity, after personal assistance to the individual constituents, the rank and file subleaders are individually more dependent upon the mayor's favor and incumbency than he is upon theirs. In any particular instance, their desires may be deferred to other orders of business. Subleaders committed to the Democratic label, for example, were disappointed over the mayor's change of party. Their disappointment did not prohibit the move.

The popular notion that these supporters are attached to the politician only by dependence and the prospect of material gain is, however, quite incomplete as a description of Sabonjian's subleaders. And Banfield's notion that the ward and precinct party leaders in Chicago can consistently be seconded to the demands of the outlying areas (the good government voters, the pressure groups) does not hold for Waukegan.[6] Sabonjian does not see the relationship between himself and his subleaders as being so asymmetrical. The unconditional support of these persons is critical to securing the cooperation he needs to be effective in building a record which will appeal to the good government forces and to bargaining with the independent community leaders. Nor are they totally dependent upon his incumbence for their positions. On the same day as he filed for office, the candidate who opposed Sabonjian in 1969 introduced himself to the corps of city employees and assured them that if elected mayor he would make no staff changes. What stake, then, do these workers have in unconditionally supporting Bob Sabonjian, and in assuming the worst of the campaign drudgery (during and between elections)? Clearly the connection between material gain and supporting one's benefactor is not so simple. And, indeed, Sabonjian does not rely only on ability to reward or remove from office to hold this support. He works long and hard to build something besides simple dependence; he works tirelessly to construct relationships of devoted gratitude, friendship and *mutual* loyalty among these workers and himself. Much of this is built through reciprocal aid (awarded against many strongly competing demands). While Sabonjian expects his subleaders to produce for him in terms of work and support—campaigning, proselytizing, and passing ordinances—he expects to see also that they get much of what they want. This is true except in cases of real emergency, when the subleaders themselves can see the emergency or in cases where they will take Sabonjian's word that the rare negative decision was necessary.

Richard Neustadt stresses the importance of a political head's firmness in his policy commitments if he is to retain the loyalty of the professionals who work under him. A vacillating president, Neustadt argues, leaves his supporters vulnerable to changing positions and weakens his hand with regard to eliciting their support.[7] In a sense, Neustadt reads policy vacillation as a betrayal of loyalty, of not taking care of one's own. Nor is the relationship between loyalty and internal reward, on the one hand, and organization efficiency, on the other, peculiar to political organization. Melville Dalton describes the use of "unofficial rewards" in industry to circumvent the inadequacies of formal organization for real production.[8] In addition to making it possible for administrators to reward exceptional contribution, the "gift" element of unofficial rewards, the human component, contributes to invaluable solidarity within the work force.

In "The Protection of the Inept," William Goode describes similar behavior for a wide array of human social organizations. He argues that objective and formal performance appraisal, when unmitigated by humanizing elements, produces insecurity among group members and results in "the undermining of group structure, the loss of the usual benefits of organization and cooperation, and the dissolution of group loyalties." Consequently such phenomena as the high evaluation of loyalty and presumption of tenure are found throughout human social organization.[9]

This is not to say that "unofficial rewards" may not become "organized theft" or that protection of the inept may not become dysfunctional for the productivity of an organization. It is simply that human organization, political or other, must consider such needs as solidarity, as well as more impersonal control systems and performance ratings.

For the political head, loyalty to one's friends is essential to strong commitments. Bob Sabonjian's relations with his sub-leaders are infused with this idea. Thus his change of party was carefully countered with protection for his friends. He made it clear that he still supported those who had been his supporters and co-workers: "Just because I have dissociated myself from the [Democratic] organization does not means that I have dissociated myself from my friends" (1-27-69). Having made this statement, he astonished party politicians by endorsing all of the incumbent aldermen—without regard to party label—and working hard for their elections.

In an earlier council election Sabonjian's loyalty to an incumbent was striking. He refused to support a Puerto Rican challenger, although the non-Puerto Rican incumbent was seriously ill, and the area was predominantly Puerto Rican. Indeed, the mayor sent letters to the residents in the ward in which he asked them to reelect the eight year incumbent. His letter mentioned the illness (the candidate died a few weeks after his reelection) and asked the people to give him their vote as a bouquet of flowers. While the mayor knew he could appoint a candidate of his choosing should the alderman be unable to carry out the job, and thereby protect his council strength, he was uncertain about the effects of his action on the unity of the Puerto Rican community and its support for him. He chose, however, to fight for the alderman, saying that he didn't know what would happen. Most important, the man had been a loyal friend through the years; if he wanted to run, the mayor would support him. (When the alderman died, the mayor appointed a Puerto Rican replacement.)

The mayor also takes care of friends who lose; he finds jobs for them elsewhere. He insists that, when at all possible, top posts in city agencies be filled by promotions from within. And there is support for those who retire. The *News-Sun* reported:

> The Waukegan City Council has been told by Mayor Robert Sabonjian to study the city's pension plan for the possibility of finding a way to include former employees in it.
> The Mayor points out that many employees retired before the present system was started and some older employees are not getting enough money to live on because they retired when salaries were very low. (5-17-69)

For subleaders who are not employed by the city, there is similar loyalty. Sabonjian works hard to find jobs for persons sponsored by cooperative ethnic leaders although this policy has been assailed by some. One Puerto Rican member of the party protesting his closeness to the established Puerto Rican leader questioned:

> Why does everything have to go through Eddy? Why can't anybody come to your office without asking him first? Why can't anybody get a job without asking Eddy? Mr. Montano this, Mr. Montano that. . . .

While this is not technically correct (others can and do come to the mayor directly), it indicates his partiality to working with Montano. For other outside leaders there is similar loyalty—whether the problem is fund raising, donations, legal advice, recommendations or credit.

Sabonjian recognizes, supports and defends subleaders. When two aldermen got into an embarrassing tangle with a construction company, Sabonjian supported them: "I want the people to understand what some of our aldermen have to put up with. As Mr. Anderson said, he has been insulted and shown disrespect and Alderman Keber was threatened" (8-8-67). When the police department came under attack, Sabonjian rose in its defense:

> "I want to go on record right now," the mayor said. "We have the best damn police department in the country. There might be one or two individuals that are on the wrong track but as a whole it is a fine department." (4-22-69)

Some forms of recognition are quite tangible. When his building commissioner died, Sabonjian spearheaded a move to have a room at the City of Hope dedicated to him. He had a Waukegan street named for an alderman who had served on the council for a thirty-one year period. Another street was named for a local restauranteur whose loyalty to Waukegan Sabonjian found outstanding (and whose restaurant was suddenly bypassed). Social ties to many of his subleaders are close. Where this is not true, the manner of relating is nevertheless warm. When, for example, the church next door to City Hall sponsored a pancake breakfast, Sabonjian rounded up two dozen city employees to eat as his guests at the church. This outing surprised no one.

Sabonjian's determination that relations with subleaders should not be simply firm but also amicable and loyal is rewarded. Although statements of intent here must be impressionistic, they seem accurate. The mood among employees attending the park board meeting in defense of the city was not one of pressure but of gratitude, friendship, and willingness to repay. When a rumor that threats had been made on the mayor's life began to circulate, one of his aldermen became almost comically insistent that the mayor have a bodyguard—if he had to take the job himself. "Robey won't let me go anywhere by myself," said the amused but touched Sabonjian. "I asked him if we could have separate beds." When a Catholic priest attacked the mayor's race policies, a black minister called to inquire about the seriousness of the charge; he said that, if the mayor liked, the black ministers would make a statement condemning the priest and supporting their friend. A group of policemen chipped in to buy a gun for the mayor's collection. After the mayor's 1969 party change and his independent endorsement of candidates, the five incumbent Democratic aldermen, three of whom were up for reelection, began a write-in campaign for the nomination of Sabonjian in the Democratic primary. A Republican alderman, not himself up for reelection in 1969, entertained the residents of a large apartment complex at a private party in honor of the mayor.

Subleaders not only go to the people for Sabonjian but bring the people back to him. They keep their eyes open and report on what they see. They are among those the mayor trusts most. Importantly, he trusts them because he interprets their actions and their reports as protective and well intended—based on their faith in, allegiance to, and identification with him.

While all of the gestures cited as indications of loyalty and good will could be read as rational gain, the gratuitous component is present and frequently dominant in such acts. Sabonjian is describing accurately his relationships with subleaders when he says:

> Loyalty is as important as anything in politics. You build it up. These are the people you know you can count on and you need each other. Over the years, they come to know that you tell them straight when you can do something and when you can't or won't. . . . I know Robey and Hugo and . . . haven't got a crooked thought in their heads. And when I ask them to go along with me on something I want, they don't ask any questions. They know that I've never steered them wrong yet. If I want something, they know I want it because I think it's good for Waukegan. Only your old friends can trust you enough to give you support like that. It takes time to build up loyalty. And I'm the same way with them. I tell

them if I don't think their plans make sense, but I end up saying: "You really want this, don't you?" And if they do, I back them up.

One of Sabonjian's subleaders, the superintendent of streets scoffed at Banfield's statement that Mayor Daley seconds the ward bosses to the outlying area residents: "He's so tight with the ward bosses they don't even have to live in the ward to be an official there. You can bet he does O.K. by them on the things they care about." Whether this is true of Chicago or not, there are indications from both leader and subleader that it is true of Waukegan.

A qualification seems in order. The relations this author personally observed between the mayor and his workers were between a mayor of ten to twelve years' incumbency and his associates. Over this length of time, he had no doubt done much to create the situation he wanted—adjusting staff and establishing precedents. Nevertheless, my observations showed little strife, and indeed enthusiastic teamwork. I saw a system the mayor must have done much to create, but I saw it at a rather mature stage. The only deviant cases were a single failure to reappoint a department head, electoral campaigns against opposition aldermen, and a verbal attack on selected appointees.

The failure to reappoint turned out to be not a hatchet job but rather the end of over-extended loyalty. Sabonjian had appointed a rather unlikely man for an understood short term. The top job had been given to the particular individual—not because of Sabonjian's faith in his continuing ability to handle the job, but precisely because of his extraordinarily long and devoted tenure on a city job and Sabonjian's desire to reward that with a term as head.

Attacks on opposition aldermen indicate Sabonjian's feeling about non-loyalty and non-cooperation and give a clue to stages in Sabonjian's political career when his work force was less unified. He responds as opponent to systematic non-cooperation on the council. At election time, he sent a personal letter to all homes in an opposition alderman's ward. The following is an example.

Dear Friend:

It isn't often that I ask you to do anything on my behalf, but I feel it is important to the best interest of our city and to the people of the 5th ward, that I ask you to help me elect a man to the office of alderman who will work toward the progress and best interests of our city, instead of being against everything.

Please understand, I feel that every person has a right to his own opinions, and has a right to disagree, but I do not feel that a person in a responsible position, such as an alderman is, should spend all his time opposing every proposal.[10]

For me to serve you best, I need someone I can work with in your ward. I have found it impossible to work with H————————, your present alderman.

Such letters have been consistently fatal to the person running against the mayor's candidate. The mayor's resource here is his personal popularity poised against that of the alderman. The alderman, too, has by this time found it difficult to respond to ward requests with city resources.

The mayor's single attack on his appointees, another case of internal strife, occurred at a council meeting where homeowners had gathered to complain about flooded basements. In an article the next day headed "Mayor Blisters Aids," the *News Sun* gave this account of the meeting.

> Obviously nettled by the criticism of the sewer system, the Mayor said: "I'm tired of sitting up here week after week and covering for you people. If you people are going to be working for the city then let's work together. I'm tired of the aldermen, the clerk, myself and the workers at the yard being out at all hours of the night while the engineers are home warm in their beds." (7-1-69)

This was the only case where Sabonjian publicly attacked his own appointees, although private demands upon subleaders are great, and in cases of disappointment his rage is also sizeable. Yet those he attacked in this statement were not subleaders but simply salaried technicians of the city government. While they in no way oppose the mayor, they are loosely related to him. They are not members of Sabonjian's team. Within the Waukegan city work force, such individuals are as rare as this single incident in thirty months would indicate.

To say that a system based on loyalty will not reward disloyalty (in, for example, allowing the disloyal to share in scarce resources) is perhaps to simply paraphrase the Machiavellian dictum that a leader must be both loved and feared, and indeed that the love is in part derived from confidence in the effectiveness and constancy of the leader on whom one relies for protection and rewards. Sabonjian, like other successful politicians, is described as both loyal and vindictive, depending on the persuasion of the observer. Both words refer to the specifically human component in a highly successful political organization.

Subleaders either allocate funds to the advantage of the executive or they do not; they either carry out directives or they refuse. Both legislatively and administratively, they can act to support or torpedo the programs of the mayor. He may inherit a more or less tight structure in established political alliances. His ability to control depends upon his ability to make alliance with him profitable and allegiance to him gratifying.

Interest Advocates Some persons are moderately independent as individuals, have reasonable alternatives in the private sphere, and are not normally interested in patronage or regularized political activity. They nevertheless have interests which they feel can be furthered through political involvement. Indeed our political culture gives private interest a public claim. Special interest involvement is not a consequence of political dependence or for the purpose of political careers. Communications with and ties to the political network are more often in terms of citizen right, just cause, or pressure group activity. This category includes private businessmen seeking zoning changes, road improvements, police patrolling, board appointments, approval for business promotions, city contracts, etc. Included also are self-appointed representatives of a cause or city "need," and the active members of the community's voluntary organizations, e.g. Downtown Waukegan Council, Grand Avenue Businessmen's Association, League of Women Voters, Chamber of Commerce, NAACP, and Small Homeowners Association.

Whether such persons seek individual or group goals, they and those they claim to represent (usually the good government voters) are what Sabonjian frequently thinks of as "troublemakers." They demand much and they demand often. The relationship is perpetually problematic. The typical form of the request is the petition; sometimes it is the placard:

> The below signed organizations who have members in your community ask that you participate in the drawing of state fair-housing legislation.

and:

> Enclosed you will find copies of published information that is relevant to an issue [parent dissatisfaction with the school board's plan

for redrawing school boundaries to establish racial balance] we feel should be of interest and importance to you. We ask for your aid in pursuing this issue. Many are concerned.

Such groups do not control resources of political importance in any significant way; those resources they do have are unorganized. These are uncertain constituencies. They are not oriented to exchange or cooperation as Sabonjian sees it, nor do they see a favor as warranting a vote—let alone loyalty or non-specific support. It is to these issue-proposing, issue-opposing, self-moving, self-aspiring organizations and individuals that Banfield attributes civic controversy in Chicago. Detailing the careers of several Chicago controversies, Banfield states that Daley watched the controversies develop and, if agreement was reached among groups, ratified that agreement; but since Daley is usually unwilling to impose a solution, most issues end in stalemate. This indeed describes a subset of mayoral politics although it by no means exhausts strategies nor even incorporates the most important. Yet, with specific regard to the conflicting positions of interest advocates (acknowledging their questionable usefulness as allies), Sabonjian fits the model Banfield draws. Like Daley, he takes a stand-off position. In Sabonjian's case, it is frequently an irritated stand-off. He will approve what does not conflict with any of his more important commitments, which include all of his other commitments.

In Waukegan, this type of controversy arose over the proposed redrawing of school boundaries to achieve racial balance. Although school boundaries were to be redrawn by the school board, Sabonjian received petitions from parents objecting to any boundary change, and to any lack of boundary change. He received petitions from parents objecting to each plan for boundary change. Disinclined to involve himself, he ignored the series of petitions. He saw petitioners as unreliable, ungrateful, and troublesome, better left to solve or stalemate their own problems.

Apathy on the part of other groups, and most importantly, on the part of the mayor's more reliable cohorts and constituents, becomes a central condition for the passage of pressure group proposals. Most zoning changes, for example, pass uncontested. Yet three times the council refused to approve zoning board changes for a nursing home when opposition developed in the neighborhood. The same has been true of proposed changes to allow multiple dwelling housing.

Insofar as the Waukegan proposal for federal urban renewal became defined as a business promotion, it caused the mayor all the problems of a special interest proposal. Yet urban renewal did not suffer from the blatant political contradictions which frequently characterize pressure group politics. First, established pressure groups were themselves in agreement; their demands were not contradictory. Secondly, the proponents of urban renewal were not persons heavy on demands and light on resources or willingness to reciprocate; they were community leaders ready and willing to contribute substantially toward the realization of the program. When the issue came to the fore, they had already commissioned and paid for several renewal plans. Yet this proposal for highly visible public action developed as threateningly partisan.

The move for urban renewal was initiated by an organization of downtown businessmen. It developed into a very controversial issue and was finally defeated in a city-wide "advisory referendum" called by the mayor. Supporters included all of the persons who, in this author's study of reputational influence, were named as top community influentials. These, in turn, were backed by the city's most visible institutional leaders and by the widest array of civic associations. The campaign for passage was well financed and hard fought. The public opposition was voiced by two transitory organizations: The Small Homeowners' Association and the Association of Collective Taxpayers. Neither of these had a membership list.

Since no tax money was involved, advocates had hoped the city council would pass the first stage of the renewal program, the downtown plan, without referendum. They were disappointed and somewhat incredulous (in view of the rare unanimity of levels and varieties of formal organization) when the mayor called the referendum. They were surprised also by his lack of support in passing the referendum. He nominally supported renewal but employed none of his well-known campaign techniques (personal contacts, letters, door-to-door canvassing) to influence favorably the outcome of the referendum. The final vote showed renewal defeated by a margin of three to one.

Asked about his position, the mayor made the following remarks:

> I thought the issue was a loser and called the referendum to get out from under.

My phone was hot all of the time with south siders calling, "Bobby, are you going to take my home?" They would have thought I was working for the merchants.

The folks just north of downtown were insulted that a bunch of businessmen should decide that their homes were blighted.

Did you ever see the Chamber of Commerce elect anyone?

Even under renewal's seemingly favorable circumstances, the mayor was unreceptive to the proposal. He saw pressure group sentiment as unrepresentative of his relevant audience, relied on his personal communications network for ascertaining opinion, and himself became the effective channel through which seemingly unorganized but politically important opinion was felt.

Analytically similar was Waukegan's several year controversy over the city's main street. Having some rather comic overtones, this issue also involved a proposal of the downtown businessmen's association. The proposal, supported by 75 percent of the downtown businessmen asked that the main shopping street be made one-way south. The chief of police, and the city engineer spoke for the plan when it was presented to the city council in July, 1967. A spokesman for the businessmen read a statement of the U. S. Chamber of Commerce which urged the use of one-way city streets. They were useful, it said, as a means of "speeding up traffic flows and taking the tedium out of long city trips."

Other supporters were attracted by the more immediate objective of the one-way proposal: the change, it was assumed, would reduce the ease with which area teenagers could "scoop the loop." "Scooping the loop" is the popular term for driving north and south on the city's main street by way of either u-turns or left turns into parking lots at the north and south ends of the single street involved. The turns make it possible for participants from all over the county to be on the same street at the same time, waving and honking at their friends. Tenants in downtown apartments complained that during evening hours, the noise was unbearable. Customers found traffic discouraging; businessmen said sales lagged. General users reported abuse. An alderman, checking complaints, reported that it had taken him eighteen minutes to cover five blocks on Genesee Street at 9 p.m. on a Saturday night.

Yet when the Downtown Waukegan Council proposed that the city adopt the one-way plan for a three month trial plan, the mayor stated that he was "unalterably opposed" to the proposal in any form. " 'I don't feel it (loop-scooping) is that big a problem' " he said. He also said that motorists coming from the south side would have to drive further in order to get onto Genesee Street (7-18-67).

The mayor remained unmovable. He responded to continuous pressure to experiment with the one-way with alternative proposals for controlling traffic. These included such plans as off-street customer parking, shutting the street off mall fashion, and expanding recreational facilities for teens. Only the mayor was overtly opposed to the one-way street proposal, but his opposition was final. As with urban renewal, he saw pressure group sentiment as unrepresentative of his relevant constituency. The latter included teenagers, their parents and the poorer south side residents who would be discommoded and insulted by discriminatory access to the city's main public space.

This is not to say that private interest advocates get nothing. They do highlight issues of concern to them, which may be of concern to others as well or may elicit indifference. Either way, pressure groups can sometimes achieve a relatively good bargaining position. Even when for government officials the political costs of implementing a proposal exceed possible gain, pressure groups may bargain for a share in a compromise agreement, e.g. businessmen may lose the one-way but persuade city officials to increase downtown parking.

But the mayor's responsiveness continues to depend upon the mayor's multiple relationships. A close associate of Chicago's Mayor Daley says Daley asks himself three questions when he is confronted with a special interest proposals. These no doubt summarize Sabonjian's concerns also. The questions are: "What can the mayor get by with in terms of the constituents?" "What is in it for the mayor?" and "Who proposes: friend, foe, neither?" The first question asks what are the minimum expectations of those Dahl calls "largely apolitical strata,"—the following, the good government voters, and the indifferent upper class? What are the bottom limits of constituent tolerance? Would downtown renewal, a highly visible action, be perceived as inimical to the interests or sympathies of "citizens" (as partisan to business interests or as acquiescent to federal control)? Would the redirecting of main street traffic be perceived by teens and south siders as discriminatory or exclusive or as improper control over public space? The pressures from the apolitical strata are indirect and not represented in some ultimate fashion by the vocal pressure groups. They are determined to work through the mayor's personal information networks, whether these be trusted and well-placed confidants or sample surveys. (Mayor Lee used the latter in New Haven.) It became clear in the urban renewal and one-way street studies that there is no necessary relationship between advocates and constituents. The views of the "largely apolitical constituents" weigh powerfully and independently of advocate pressure.

Daley's second question—"What's in it for the mayor?"—asks why the mayor should bother to expend his resources. First, what will be the consequences of action in terms of results and probable responses to them? Second, what resources will become available to the mayor as a consequence of expending resources now? This raises the question of timing—gaps of time between expenditure of resources and benefits as these relate to other pressures and to the political timetable. The answer to this question is intimately related to the third question: "Who proposes: friend, foe or neither?" This is scarcely more than a restatement of the second question since calculating expenditure and estimating gain cannot be disentangled from judging the commitment, the trustworthiness and the reliability of associates. Issue-oriented head-counting as a way of predicting executive decision is vacuous for heads do not count equally. How firm will be the reciprocation and how generalizeable over issues? This question raised by Sabonjian in discussing loyalty and the importance of "old friends," ties the present vividly to the past and the future since the past provides the only relevant data for predictions and since actions today have important consequences for the commitments of tomorrow.

As an example of this all-important third answer, Daley's associate cited two Chicago real estate ventures indicating the difference he felt the source of a proposal made. The first was the building of Marina Towers on the Fort Dearborn site. When a Daley teammate, an old and loyal buddy of the mayor's (a prominent labor Republican) proposed to build the Towers under his direction and with money from the janitors' union, the mayor responded with support and assistance. He facilitated the necessary zoning at the choice Chicago River site. He provided city help in preparing the riverside land, and corrected problems which made construction difficult. (This, incidentally was the proposed site of the business-supported Fort Dearborn Project, the failure of which Banfield documents in *Political Influence*.) When a Philadelphia businessman proposed the building of Chicago's tallest building, the giant Hancock Center, the mayor was, while not opposed, by and large neutral. The construction problems and delays on this building were so frequent that the businessman, handling them without help from the mayor, went broke and was forced to sell the building before its completion.

With regard to each of the mayor's concerns, pressure groups usually perform badly. They seek public solutions for problems which are apt to be partisan in nature and disagreeable to other pressure groups and to other constituents. Although these examples were somewhat atypical, pressure groups generally contribute little. Fractionated, they do not control important resources. Most importantly, their ideological or interest group orientation is apt to interfere with supra-issue loyalty, commitments over time and, as a consequence, with their political value. Says Sabonjian: "You can't cooperate with people who won't cooperate."

It is useful to note that when subleaders take on pressure group tactics, the mayor responds accordingly. When several aldermen turned in lists of requests for improvements in their wards, Sabonjian admonished:

> I respect you as people but I want you to read *Roberts Rules of Order* as to what an alderman is. We're running a city not a ward. You guys are all trying to be administrators, trying to match one ward against another. Lists of requests and demands for a survey aren't going to get us anywhere. . . .

Conversely, potential interest advocates may become quasi-subleaders. When members of voluntary organizations or boards feel there is sufficient advantage to be gained from solid support of the mayor they can provide valuable help in achieving representation and success in hard-to-control regions of activity. Thus in the case of the civic center, the mayor's friends on the park board, by their early support of the land grant to the city, saved him work and helped to place pressure on more reluctant members to acquiesce. (Only one of the mayor's park board subleaders was a current city official; one was a retired city employee, one was a high school teacher.) In the same way, subleaders in voluntary organizations propose and fight for organization endorsements of candidates and city programs. Finally, for those who invest loyalty, larger donations than would be predicted by sheer size of operation can be elicited for causes which might not interest the real monied interests. Thus, while the mayor's subleaders set about selling their allotted fractions of the one thousand one-dollar raffle tickets Sabonjian had agreed to sell for a Puerto Rican Society Raffle, the mayor contacted persons in contracting, building and road material, architecture, and liquor businesses who bought the bulk of the tickets. His superintendent of streets contacted additional persons in trucking and tire sales; members of the building department sold to plumbing firms, a chemical corporation, air-conditioning and electrical firms. Similarly Sabonjian recruited real estate brokers to purchase tickets he had agreed to sell for a local semi-pro football team and for a black church fundraising event.

As a boost to the mayor's beautification program, area organizations of contractors and cement finishers built and donated a fountain which they located across from the new civic center site. The contractors joined the Waukegan Exchange Club in contributing also a band shell for the Waukegan Beach. A cement firm paid for developing and framing pictures taken of the council members at a ribbon-cutting ceremony.

Which members of the moderately autonomous, largely private sphere, middle group volunteer or can be recruited to work dependably for political purposes? In some cases the logic is clear. In the case of contractors and other persons associated with the building industry, the private game in which they are engaged is scarcely more independent of political favor (given government control over zoning, road usage, inspections, and licenses as well as city contracts) than are government careers. In Illinois, where the mayor by state law has personal control over liquor licenses and where the council has control over closing hours, persons in the liquor industry are similarly dependent. To others, however, reappointment to a particular board is more important than the issues the board considers. Some participate because they like the mayor; some like the political game. These are the middle-class subleaders. They, like the less autonomous subleaders, approve, donate, support.

The clear relationships of mutual help between the mayor and these moderately autonomous subleaders must not be overstated. Sabonjian defended many persons and businesses with whom no relationship was perceptible. In the absence of conflict with other commitments, the mayor's impulse is protective. Moreover, Sabonjian, a small businessman before beginning his career in politics, is committed to assisting hard work and independent effort. He sees hard work and self-reliance as the road to individual and group prosperity and as the cure for social ills. Thus, he is protective not only of friends but of effort as well. When he says to a person applying for a liquor license: "I'll save one for you, but not at that location. All you'd be doing would be dividing up the business," he seems to mean it in an ideological as well as a political sense. Similarly, his standard answer to questions regarding social policy is "Everybody's working, aren't they?" and "If somebody wants a job, I'll find him one. I never let anybody down who wants to work."

Institutional Dominants Standing at institutional peaks, highly autonomous participants are characterized by their independent resources of power. These are the persons who possess independent and substantial control over such resources as 1) money and credit, 2) jobs, 3) the information of others, 4) social standing, 5) knowledge and expertise, 6) popularity, esteem, charisma, 7) legality, constitutionality, officiality, 8) ethnic solidarity, 9) the right to vote.[11]

In the compilation of a list of Waukegan's reputed influentials, the thirty-four persons receiving the most nominations were all professionals, self-employed businessmen owning large and prosperous business, or high level managers and officials (See Table III).[12] They constituted a category of persons whose access to resources could not be revoked or undercut by the disfavor of the mayor. Only two persons besides the mayor (a bank president and the publisher of the newspaper) were nominated by all respondents. Many others were nominated by substantial fractions. The first eighteen on the list were interviewed.

TABLE III
INFLUENTIALS IN WAUKEGAN BY OCCUPATIONAL POSITION, 1966
N=34

INFLUENTIALS RANK	VOTES RECEIVED	POSITION
1	23	Mayor
1	23	Bank President
1	23	Newspaper Publisher
2	15	Assistant to the Publisher
2	15	Executive V.P. Manufacturing Co. (5200 employees in Waukegan)
3	10	Retired Executive V.P. Manufacturing Co. (3200 employees)
3	10	Executive V.P. Pharmaceutical Co. (5400 employees)
4	8	Owner and President of 3 small manufacturing co.'s (50 employees)
4	8	Owner and President, Department Store
4	8	Owner and Pres., Department Store
4	8	Appellate Court Judge
5	7	Catholic Priest
5	7	Juvenile Court Judge
5	7	Owner & Pres., Men's Store
6	6	Physician (private office)
6	6	Municipal Corporation Counsel
6	6	Township Supervisor
6	6	Owner & Pres., Finance Co.
7	5	Executive V.P. under 2 above (for local plant)
7	5	Superintendent of Schools
8	4	City Clerk
8	4	Federal Court Judge
9	3	U. S. Congressman
9	3	Owner & Pres., retail store
9	3	State Senator
9	3	Attorney (private office)

9	3	Pres., Real Estate Co.
10	2	Minister Baptist Church
10	2	Circuit Court Judge
10	2	Professional Attorney (private)
10	2	Retired Union Representative
10	2	Attorney (private office)
10	2	Owner & Pres., retail store
10	2	Manager Chain Dept. Store

When asked what steps they would take to realize a proposal, these men said they would contact others on the list for support. Without at least the consent of the three top influentials, a proposal would have little chance. Yet, none of the dominants cited the demands of other leaders as important to his personal participation. Nor did any mention political associations, loyalties or dependencies. Instead, answers were concerned with public obligations, worthy causes and maintaining organizational viability.

Persons giving the last response referred specifically to stability in the relationships and arrangements which constitute their private bases of power. Both respondents from the newspaper stated that the newspaper participation represented obligation of the newspaper to the organizations which support it. Both said that the newspaper grew as the city grew. A financier saw a prosperous community as a key to property values. An elected judge, a practicing lawyer, and a priest saw community service as ways of meeting potential clients. Industrial executives expressed an interest in broad community-related labor problems (migration patterns, vocational training) and in determining the transportation networks which service industrial areas. These statements are functionally analogous to the mayor's most important concerns. Where the mayor relies on constituents and subleaders for security and power, the newspaper publishers rely on readers and supporting organizations, and the financier looks to property values. The judge was concerned with constituents and judicial colleagues; the Catholic priest was concerned with his congregation and the lawyer with his clients; the industrialists were concerned with industrial needs.

Leaders cooperate with but do not control one another. Each, including the mayor, is aware that so long as one man holds a position of power, other leaders will have to deal with him as an equal. Neither institutional self-interest nor personal standards need be compromised. Nor can a dominant afford compromise in such vital areas. The mayor was able to elicit the support of subleaders in behalf of the civic center, but not of other leaders. The newspaper would not endorse the project and necessary financial support was lacking. By the same token, influentials, when organized as a pressure group for urban renewal (urban renewal required council passage), were no more successful than other pressure groups in securing government action. The reputational power structure came out in force; the mayor was unresponsive. A politically enfranchised constituency provided effective nd decisive limits on the ability of economic elites to effect public policy.

The translation of one type of power into another (e.g., economic into political) is problematic and can be understood only within a particular institutional context. In the case of urban renewal, the mayor's most stable commitments were threatened. He could have pleased important economic and social interests in the city, but he sensed too much displeasure from his constituents. "Did you ever see the chamber of commerce elect anyone?" Presumably the strategies of other dominants also incorporate commitments not visible to the outsider but prescribed by organizational roles.

It is success in private projects, incidentally, and not influence over government, which causes non-political influentials to receive influence nominations. In Waukegan, there are many examples of the ability and willingness of persons in this category to pursue goals through private means. Where political action may well be the only available route for subleaders and pressure groups to achieve group or community goals, community leaders can often achieve similar results independently or with small, easy to obtain authorization from the city. After the defeat of urban renewal in Waukegan, for example, downtown merchants combined privately owned customer parking lots into free "city" lots so that customer shopping could take on the plaza mood; they decorated the backs of their stores to make entrance from the lots more pleasant and they paid $110,000 for a lighting system. Another move was the purchase and staffing of a $300,000 parking lot which is leased to the city for one dollar a year. Such actions could have been, but were not, defined as public rather than private endeavors.

Influence nominations draw out awareness of the more or less "private" issues which are decided daily by interested and institutionally important persons. A limited group of persons are named because limited types of people, be it largely in the playing of private games, continue to make decisions which have broad or dramatic community impact.[13] It is interesting that the mayor's influence nominations differed in important respects from those given by other influentials; unlike the other lists which emphasized financial and excluded political leaders (other than the mayor), half of the mayor's nominations were ethnic leaders.

Because their interests are community wide, institutional dominants with quite different bases of power will find that their interests often converge. The political game, the business game, the industry game, the banking and newspaper games frequently require a common concern with such things as city image, as it appears to a prospective new industry which could bring in jobs, employees, shoppers, money-borrowers and newspaper readers. Many dominants desire a new shopping mall, a more attractive, more profitable downtown, a better trained labor force, a richer or more literate public. While businessmen, industrial executives, politicians, and other institutional leaders differed (by institutional affiliation) in their selection of key issues, all named the needs of the industries, the economic base, as first.

The mayor and the chamber of commerce work hard at recruiting new industry. With executives of Outboard Marine Corporation, the newspaper, and the port authority, the mayor worked to annex a piece of state-owned park for a Waukegan marina. In cooperation with the downtown businessmen, the mayor found ways to ease parking problems in the downtown area. He worked with the newspaper publisher and economic dominants in the battle to retain the Courthouse complex in Waukegan and to incorporate the site of Lakehurst shopping mall. He continued to work with economic and civic groups in the recruiting of new industries to the city. In these enterprises all have contributions to make. Because of the need to coordinate resources, there is mutual advantage in cooperation among leaders. Customary channels develop to handle such coordination. But such persons are likely to cooperate only so long as their private interests or beliefs are enhanced by the arrangement. Thus appeals among leaders must be made in terms of reason, self-interest, and/or community benefit—not loyalty or dependence. Bargaining, persuasion, reasoning, and selling are the tactics used to secure cooperation among the politically autonomous.

Some analysts make this clear. Dahl tells us that New Haven's powerful Mayor Lee could not force the school superintendent to comply with his wishes on an important school issue.[14] Nor could he force the influential members of the Citizens' Action Commission to sponsor Urban Renewal. The mayor could appeal to the CAC only by convincing members that the proposals "made sense according to their own predispositions," for "the men on the CAC were too important in their own right, too knowledgeable, and too independent to be merely tools of the Mayor."[15] Similarly, Banfield argues that the powerful *Tribune* could not force Daley to comply with its wishes. In selling the idea of the McCormick Place Exposition Center to the mayor, the *Tribune's* managing editor relied on his belief that "Any mayor would be soft in the head not to want an improvement like that for his city."[16] Unlike the *Tribune* editor, Chicago businessmen failed to convince Mayor Daley that it was in his own best interest to sponsor the Fort Dearborn Project (*their* idea for developing the Chicago River bank). Sponsorship was not forthcoming and they could in no way require it.[17]

A Waukegan example of the process whereby independent evaluation of rational interest did produce cooperation was the development of the move to have the Waukegan area declared a Standard Metropolitan Statistical Area separate from Chicago SMSA. The idea was first proposed by the newspaper publisher whose original interest was to bring in for his newspaper and radio station the national advertising which is awarded only to metropolitan regions. The mayor was from the beginning agreeable to requesting the new statistical designation. Unlike urban renewal, this proposal appeared to be non-controversial, thus a costless means for achieving small gains; "Greater Waukegan" had a nice ring to it, and it would please the publisher. The mayor put in the request. It took more for him to begin a real drive to acquire the designation. Real interest emerged when he learned of additional advantages which would accompany the designation. These advantages, including government aid in long-range home financing for moderate-income families, enhanced chances for federal aid in park and other expansion programs, and marketing assistance for commercial interests, were pet interests of the mayor. Profit loomed larger. He joined advocates and petitioned personally in Washington.

Sabonjian communicates with community "influentials" very infrequently, not simultaneously, and only with regard to specific projects. "We only occasionally work together," he said, "But then, we work like hell." Organizing resources for concerted action requires this notion of common gain although low cost may be determinative in Sabonjian's willingness to perform small favors when gains are not important but losses are fewer. This proposition describes the mayor's early reaction to applying for Metropolitan status. There are other cases as well. The city council unanimously awarded the CATV (Community Antenna T.V.) franchise to the News-Sun Broadcasting Company. The mayor breakfasted with the United Fund Board when requested to do so by the executive vice president of a large manufacturing firm. He agreed to go with the bank president and other members of the Minority Housing Commission to look at sites for housing. Sabonjian does not appear to refuse this type of low-cost cooperation with community leaders. On the other hand, it is difficult to separate his response to requests from influentials and his response to similar requests from other persons in the community, or to exclude action based on his notion of what is worthwhile or good for the city and what is not. Sabonjian assists small businessmen as well as the newspaper in securing franchises and he works on many fund raising drives and welfare programs. While he has refused to act on some private interest requests and has not refused community leaders, the requests from the latter were so infrequent as to be altogether inconclusive in the course of this study. There is, nevertheless, a significant difference between the mayor's relations with advocate groups and those with institutional dominants, for there is another type of political advantage which is available to the politician who cooperates with the holders of powerful resources. The ability of the latter to supply very large investment, to finance or in other ways realize very large programs, tends to create the conditions where leader interest will converge with political interest. This is infrequently true of cooperation with the less powerful private interest groups—although costs to the mayor are similar. Assuming no serious demand for compromise of principle on the part of the politician or loss of public faith, the strength of the resource base from which one acts is important. Neither private groups nor community leaders are dependent upon the politician; unlike the subleaders, neither is valued for loyal support. In the case of leaders, however, there are compensating rewards for the politician who can find ways to cooperate.

Zoning changes are a striking example. Although zoning changes occur weekly and neighborhood protest is frequent, there were only two occasions where this observer witnessed Sabonjian insist on changes over citizen opposition. In each case stakes had risen far above the norm. Resource balance had collapsed, with the neighborhood values losing. Homeowners were no match for ten and thirteen million dollar, 550–600 unit developments. Sabonjian and other officials saw the latter as important additions to the city (where complexes rarely exceed 100 units) and part of the solution to housing shortage. Similarly economic dominants donate parking lots to the city, finding such influence over land use cheap.

Just as varying resource inputs from non-political leaders can alter strategies in the mayor's game, so can strength in the mayor's office alter the strategies of other games. The mayor who preceded Sabonjian was a more obliging friend to business but could not produce results in the council or on the streets. Even though he will not always do so, the mayor's ability to assure efficient services, produce council approval and measure community pressures makes him a valuable ally when interests do converge. Indeed it warrants some dispensation. "We can work with the mayor" said one industrialist, "and he can work with the town." Even when he will not activate it toward a desired goal, Sabonjian's citizen infrastructure is valuable to persons interested in public opinion, violence, labor turnover, and a controllable future. His ability to assure council approval of such things as housing, amenities, tax arrangements, and utility lines are valuable in recruiting prospective industrial, retail, or public interests to the city. The previous administration had not accomplished these things.

In discussing the politician's relationships to pressure groups on the one hand and community leaders on the other, the conditions of overlap should be noted in that resources are related to goals and demands. In ideal form, private interest advocates deal neither from the strength of dependence nor from the strength of power based on independent resources. On the other hand, real solidarity is a resource of great political importance. Organized forces which can produce in terms of delivering the vote or other political resources (work, money) can use solidarity as a base from which to bargain collectively. The Puerto Rican Society wields the power of organized voting numbers. In Waukegan, no other groups (e.g. political parties, black organizations, labor unions) have sufficient unity or organization to be able (through directing votes or mobilizing political action) to use member solidarity as a political resource across issues and over time. Given the strength of their political organization, the Puerto Ricans can expect considerable return for their support, and they get it. When, for example, black groups protested the appointment of a Puerto Rican to an unexpired aldermanic term, the mayor replied frankly (and pointedly) that he felt he owed something to the Puerto Rican community (8-15-67).

There are times when institutional dominants fail to be effective; they can frequently raise high the rewards of cooperation, but not always high enough. They are ineffective in achieving public policies which are opposed (or thought to be opposed) by constituents. In such cases, they fail for the same reason advocate interests fail. Their resources are not sufficient to make enactment of the particular policy profitable. Veto groups prevail.

The mayor's group environment is complex. The message for advocates is clear. At the level of interest, exchange balance must be achieved. One would, therefore, increase organization to the point where real power is involved (e.g. independent action can be taken, a real majority or reliable minority can be presented to political officials, or large scale contributions can be made). Alternatively, one would be advised to decrease demands.

CONSTITUENTS AND CLIENTS

The large body of constituents which is roused to political attention only by controversy plays a role, but an indirect one, in the day-to-day activities of the mayor. Those who are involved in daily politics participate primarily as clients. A population of such clients is constant, though it consists of changing individuals.

Following Like the subleaders, the low autonomy, non-participants do not have independent means of economic or social security. Their opportunities for achieving success in the private sphere are restricted; their choices are limited. They are more apt than persons higher on the socio-economic scale who have attractive alternatives in the private sphere to see political recourse as a means of securing individual ends.[18] Unlike the subleaders, these low autonomy persons are not repetitively involved in political activity. Their political recourse is manifested either in allegiance to a leader (ethnic, race, organizational) who deals for them with the political network, or in seeking direct help from political figures (precinct captain, mayor). Typically the form of request deals with obtaining a job, or some form of legal aid. Persons with small social worlds and little education seek help from their politicians in dealing with little understood economic and legal structures.

Perhaps 70 percent of the mayor's day is spent in hiring or locating jobs for the unemployed. The fact that most requests are from unskilled workers is one reason the mayor is able to process applicants so quickly. He wastes no time matching skills to jobs. Sabonjian believes that the prosperity and stability of his city depends upon a high rate of employment. Nevertheless, his personal handling of job distribution has another effect. As Mayor Daley has said, "Looking back, you never forget the person who helped you get your first job."[19] Daley's statement may have a false ring to persons with greater social alternatives and greater political awareness. Yet this loyalty is precisely the reason the following is valuable to the politician. It is a constant. Sabonjian gets letters years later from persons who appreciated his help in obtaining a job.

Legal problems are the second large area where low resource persons seek help from political figures. On several occasions persons unable to read English requested help in simply reading legal notices they had received. On frequent occasions persons confused by credit agreements, cheated by crooked salesmen or abused by landlords brought their problems to the mayor. He put his attorney on the problem or made the necessary calls himself. Persons brought pleas to the mayor asking him to keep family breadwinners out of jail or find them the jobs necessary for parole. Although in such cases the mayor was cautious, he always sought the facts of the case and usually attempted to help, if not by obtaining the jail release by finding some means of family support.

On a few occasions, persons sought help from the mayor in obtaining job guarantees in order to bring relatives from other countries into the United States. One particularly comic incident occurred when a woman requested the mayor to reclaim a sawed-off shot gun the police had confiscated. The police had been called, she said, when a friend to whom she was showing the gun mistakenly thought she was trying to kill him. Run-ins with the county government are also thought to be within the domain of the mayor. A tearful restaurateur brought his problem with the Lake County Health Inspector to the mayor. He had invested, he said, all of his savings in a small restaurant which he planned to open Monday. Now the Lake County Health Department told him he had to purchase his equipment from a different company. A friend told him the mayor would help. Whatever the final result, the mayor did give the case to his attorney and he assured the man it would work out O.K.

Hardship cases are another time consumer. Just as Boss Crump of Tennessee would send checks to families when their homes burned, Sabonjian will personally buy groceries and pay rent for needy families.[20] He lends money without interest to overextended persons and encourages them to pay their other debts first. If, when he asks, the mayor find that a man for whom he has located a job does not have bus fare to get to the job, he will have a city employee drive the man to the plant or give him the bus fare out of his own pocket. He will go to bat for followers who claim job discrimination by private employers or landlords.

Most hardship cases concern public aid. Although Sabonjian has to refer these persons (except housing) to the county office, he is available personally with the right information and the proper introductions. The following letter, for example, came to the mayor.

Dear Sir:

Once again I must ask you for your help. I suppose you have forgotten me. I am the girl who came to you to help me obtain a job.

Since talking and writing you I have had more problems.

I should have told you, at first that I was unable to work, but I had faith in you, and I thought perhaps you could somehow help me get a job, but facing facts as they are I had to go to the public

aid for help. . . . I was approved but so far they will only give
me. . . .

The mayor responded.

> Dear Mrs. ————:
>
> I was sorry to hear of the problems you have had with your public
> aid payments. This area is however beyond my jurisdiction. If you
> contact the township supervisor, Mr. August Cepon, and explain
> your situation to him, he may be able to help. His office is in the
> Lake County Building, County and Madison Streets, Waukegan.
>   I regret that I am unable to help you personally and hope that
> you will be able to work something out with Mr. Cepon. I would
> be interested in hearing how it turns out.
>
>   Sincerely,

Sabonjian not only responds as best he can to requests from persons lacking money, skills, or information. He frequently takes
the initiative in their behalf. When a man applying for a job explained that he had a bad back as a result of an accident on his
last job, Sabonjian took it upon himself to see that a suit was
brought against the company. On several occasions it was the
mayor's personal discovery that children were in need of medical
attention that resulted in charity house calls by the city physician.
Overall, persons in this category are the prime recipients of personal mayoral assistance. Personal responsiveness to individual
requests is a potent political strategy in dealing with lower autonomy persons. First, their low socio-economic status means that
support can be won through relatively low-cost response, if not
simply friendship. Second, the ethnic and neighborhood identifications which characterize many of these voters make possible the
generalizing of this "friendship" base at no cost at all. Given the
solidarity of the Puerto Ricans in Waukegan, for example, a favor
for one Puerto Rican may predictably produce a substantial
amount of support from other Puerto Ricans who accept Bob Sabonjian as "their" friend because he is their countryman's friend.
Finally, these persons are schooled in neither the morality of good
government nor the importance, however serious in fact, of issue
voting. Thus, support won from these groups tends to be stable
over time. Assuming some minimum level of consistency is main-

tained so as not to give the appearance of having betrayed one's friends, once-won support here is the most reliable in the city and therefore very carefully nurtured.

Precisely because the normal costs to the politician of maintaining a reliable following are lower with respect to the following, this group receives significant consideration when commitments conflict. This is true on higher cost demands as well as the daily requests, so long as large-scale demands do not occur too often. In that case the "following" in terms of costs, would resemble the volatile mass of "independent," "good government" voters. Such consideration is evident in several choice situations. Sabonjian took very seriously, indeed, the attitudes of his south side following in his decision against the one-way street and downtown urban renewal. Over stiff objections he appointed a Puerto Rican to finish an unexpired aldermanic term. When serious discussions began on a plan to build a highway through razed slum housing, Sabonjian was quoted repeatedly as saying that "The main problem facing Waukegan in the highway plan is the relocation of residents who would be displaced by the Lakefront Expressway" (7-11-69).[21] He fought with the housing authority over several cases where he thought racial discrimination was involved. The mayor was uninterested in a potential secretary although he liked her very much: "I like to give jobs to kids who need the money."

In the literature, low autonomy voters are rarely given much attention. They are assumed to be party voters with the party seen as a dying institution, or simply of little importance because of their low political awareness and normally small election turnout. While generalizing from Waukegan to other communities may be precarious, it is quite clear that Sabonjian, in both overt and covert dealings, courts these groups. Admittedly few *issues* reach the level of intensity needed to arouse opposition here, but those which do seem to be decided in the belief that commitments to lower class followings are sacred. Certainly, he extends and overextends himself in responding to the personal requests of these persons.

In explaining this political logic the nature of the following comes across as a voting bloc. Unlike the good government forces which demand much and promise little in return (except constant reevaluation of political performance and selective support), the support of low autonomy, non-participants can be maintained at relatively low cost. Non-participating analogue to the loyal sub-leaders, voters in the following can be counted on to turn in substantial electoral margins for Bob Sabonjian while the sub-leaders can be expected to arrange their transportation to the polls. Control over numbers is the uniquely political means by which an individual may acquire community influence. The base Sabonjian uses in dealing with the holders of such resources as publicity, knowledge, or finance is his popularity with voters and his continued incumbency in office. Some solid base of reliable support is essential if the fortunes of the politician are not to vary by the hour of the day; this is the place where it can be created at a feasible cost.

Other political leaders may compete with the mayor for the control of numbers. Insofar as another leader acquires such control, there is less slack in the system of influence available to the mayor for inclusion within his system of influence. He must negotiate with leaders of unified groups in the same way that he must negotiate with persons holding comparable resources in other realms of activity. As long as this type of counter organization is not successful or prevalent, there is more opportunity for a leader such as the mayor to enlarge his own sphere of influence.

Banfield predicts the coming of personality politics with his view of the lamentable death of the political machine. He sees personality politics as a highly unstable, highly unrepresentative approach to political action. Its result, he feels, will be politics geared to the irresponsible whim of a volatile public opinion. Sabonjian's intense commitment to maintaining support in what might, in another day, have been machine wards, suggests that in municipal politics the political principle behind the machine may die more slowly than its big city prototype. Sabonjian, at least, in spite of a complete absence of party machinery, is still very much concerned with the need for constant and dependable support. While the tactics of securing such support may vary, the importance of securing the most votes at the least cost provides an advantage of sorts to these least autonomous and most "political" elements of the population.

Good Government Voters   Although the moderately independent, politically indifferent middle is the largest category of voters, it is rarely a political force. For the most part, its members do not seek private gain through political channels and are little concerned with the public interest. They can be activated when their narrower interests are involved, particularly when they are threatened, but organization is variable, sporadic, and issue-oriented. The widely threatening urban renewal issue, for example, produced a town full of one-shot activists, responding to assumptions that urban renewal would take homes and displace persons, that it would install black housing units in white neighborhoods, that it would tax private citizens for the purpose of subsidizing downtown business and so on. Upon the appearance of the proposal such largely unknown organizations as the Association of Collective Taxpayers, and The Small Homeowners' Association suddenly burgeoned, producing great unrest and widespread interest in political pressure. *Ad hoc* citizens' groups, for and against, appeared everywhere, most of them seeking to protect private interests. While this is occasionally true of the persons in the following, the potential of small-scale citizen opposition seems greater and yet more picayune in subject among the middle. They are more independent; they are more inclined to think in terms of political right; they are more concerned with the protection of the *status quo*.

Unlike their more independent counterparts, the indifferent upper class, they are not secure enough in their claims to ignore status threat or independent enough to seek private alternatives. Once again as with the organized interest advocates, they are a trouble spot. In Sabonjian's view they are not particularly useful supporters. Their vote is not reliable and their exchange offers are negligible. Yet their claims, issued in the form of individual or group protest can be troublesome.

Said Sabonjian of a ward filled with skilled workers and white collar employees:

> That's really a crazy ward—cheese and cracker millionaires—people who have got a little bit of money and think they're real big shots. *Those* are the *real* champions of the *status quo*. They don't want to change *anything*. Everything just like it is. No progress: no shopping plazas, no apartment buildings, no row houses, no airport. . . . When I put the land-fill in over there, I had a subpoena for my arrest on my desk the next morning.

What does he do about these groups? Quoting Sabonjian again:

That's when you play politics. You bide your time. Timing becomes really important. I won't do anything until the election is over. Just wait it out. Then when you've got four years, you get through the programs you need to. By the time the four years are up they won't be holding it against me. They'll see I was right before I have to run again. But nothing controversial in those wards before an election. For now, I'll just sit it out and let them haggle all they want.

The two cases in my study where Sabonjian acted against citizen organization, the landfill and the apartment development, were in this ward and were characterized by these circumstances.

While actual change may be anathema, good government voters place far and away the most housekeeping demands—sewer repair, garbage pick-up, noise, mosquito abatement, odor elimination, and law enforcement. Good government, says the middle-class independents, is low cost, community-serving government. Good administration. Complaints—not requests as are more common from the city's south side—come overwhelmingly from the "cheese and cracker millionaires" into the mayor's office. The following examples (all predictable locations) may set the mood.

Our neighbors next door are four bachelors and they just don't care about taking care of their garbage and it's all over the place and I don't think people should have to put up with something like that. So I called the health department but that awful sanitation commissioner or whatever he's called—What's his name?—he told me there isn't anything the city can do. So I want to tell the mayor because citizens shouldn't have to put up with that.

I live at ———— and I would like the mayor to know that the citizens out here are being eaten alive by mosquitos. We think that with the taxes we pay the city should be able to supply us with some minimum level of public service. . . .

My husband and I have a hedge we work hard to keep looking nice. Twice now the mosquito abatement crew has sprayed and ruined it. We requested the city to repair or replace it and got no action. We insist that the mayor come out here and see what a mess his workers have made of our property.

My children are being harassed on their way to school by a group of older boys. We think the police in this town should be able to guarantee our children's safety on their way to and from school.

My sewer is not draining because of the debris washed back into it during the rain storm. I pay $400.00 taxes in this town and I think the city should get over here and clean it out.

I am sick and tired of cleaning my basement after water backs up from this town's faulty sewers. Unless the mayor gets his crews over here to clean my basement I will file a suit against the city and I will go to the newspapers with the story and. . . .

We moved into this neighborhood under the assumption that the zoning regulations had some importance. Therefore we assume that the authorities are not aware that our neighbor at —— is breaking zoning regulations by repairing T.V.'s in his home.

We built our houses in a sparsely populated area under the assumption that the rest of the houses in the area would be new and up to standards. We put a lot into our houses and now we find that a run down shack is being moved in. . . . Certainly the residents of an area should be consulted before the city issues a permit for a house to be moved into a neighborhood.

I couldn't get my branches out during clean-up week because I was ill. Now the city yards say they won't pick them up. I pay $400.00 taxes and I want the service I'm entitled to.

Letters of complaint regarding city services sometimes run ten pages. Compare the tone of these following letter with that from the public aid recipient a few pages back.

While Sabonjian's general strategy is to respond to these complaints, given that response doesn't cost much and may achieve something, his faith that he will receive gratitude is weak. These people have rights! His general idea seems to be that prompt personal response will convey an image of himself as a model of efficiency and other public virtues. Sabonjian's only direct telephone line to another city department is to the street department which handled the bulk of these complaints.

Quite apart from winning the *devotion* of a following there is the importance of maintaining an equilibrium with forces of good government. Sabonjian believes basic service to be the first step in creating good will. He made the following remark in response to a question concerning labor-management relations. It is probably indicative of his own position.

Some guy, Tom, comes to work every day and gets a draft changing [his clothes] because of a broken window in the locker room. So this guy raises a big fuss. He screams and yells. So the guys say: "Well at least Tom ain't afraid to speak up." So this blowhard Tom gets elected, because of that window. The next thing you know it goes to his head and he's demanding a whole new line of equipment.

What the guys wanted was for management to repair that damn window.

Mayor Daley's Office of Inquiry and Information where persons register problems corresponding to at least the range of problems mentioned here is known for its swift service. It will direct residents to the office which will see that their garbage is collected, that their landlord repairs the ceiling, that their trees are trimmed, or that their neighborhood is patrolled. "Don't worry if they're Democrats or Republicans," Mayor Daley told *Newsweek* (April 15, 1963). "Give them service and they'll be Democrats."

On the more general level, Sabonjian works tirelessly to convey an image of the entire city government as capable and efficient. His police and fire departments are well-paid, well-staffed, and well-run. One of his first projects was a program of highly effective extermination to rid the city of the rats which had become entrenched in ravines throughout Waukegan. Visible, but not controversial, public improvements have multiplied at a frantic pace to the delight of this general public. Roads and parks, beach pavillions, flower beds—most people think the city does look better. Importantly, most improvements have come from sales tax funds, motor fuel tax funds or business-industry investment rather than higher real estate taxing.

Sabonjian deals with the general middle mostly through swift service, visible evidence of efficient administration, and apparent absence of conflict, danger, crime, and unrest. There are, however, members of the middle who make personal requests and respond with loyalty to responsiveness; favors appropriate to their tastes can be obtained. His daily round of benefaction includes dispensing summer jobs to college students (450 in 1968), arranging for race track passes or dinner resrevations, issuing proclamations, conducting Brownie Scout Tours, and on and on.

When a local boy with a middle-class address wrote from Viet Nam requesting American and Illinois Flags, the mayor paid personally for their purchase and their shipping. When a sailor requested a book available through Abbott Laboratories, Sabonjian put in a request with the executive vice president who had it sent to the boy. When Sabonjian received a letter from a couple who sought his help in acquiring information on a property they owned in the county, he was quick to reply. He ordered his corporation counsel to look into the matter and send the needed information; he dictated a personal letter indicating what action he had taken.

As with the "quasi subleaders" the middle-class "quasi following" is something Sabonjian cultivates. Its members are self-selected; but Sabonjian rates high the gratitude of the middle-class mother who to her death appreciates that summer job he found for her son. For persons normally unconcerned and perhaps never concerned with issues, this kind of favor, once performed, is reason enough for a perennial vote in the right box. And, in practical terms, this is what the politician's relationship to the constituents is all about.

The scale of personalized relations here, as with the following, is phenomenal. A class of twenty-eight third graders in the most troublesome ward (where 24 of the 28 fathers were skilled laborers) were asked how many of them knew the mayor. The whole class had toured his office. Thirteen could cite specific contacts between their parents and the mayor. Two fathers got city jobs through the mayor. One had called the mayor to complain about a neighbor burning trash in the yard; one called because persons were dumping garbage in the ravine adjoining the family's house; one called to get a hose for the family's four-foot pool; one called about trespassing dogs. A mother went to the mayor's office to give him her opinion of rioters. Two families had visited the mayor's office. With two other families the mayor had struck up street conversations. One Mexican father had called the mayor when he was assaulted on the street. "The mayor got them too!" the child reported. According to their children, the other parents were similarly satisfied with their response from the mayor—although several of the reports involved parents objecting to the behavior of neighbors, something Sabonjian will not normally handle.

Interviews with twenty-six fifth graders in a somewhat wealthier area indicate predictable movement along the autonomy continuum. This school includes areas of higher autonomy constituents. Occupations of fathers included the professions, industrial management, and private business. Twenty-one of these children said their parents knew the mayor, but mention of personal favors dropped to two, (zoning variation for private pool, summer job for brother). Several fathers had professional acquaintanceships (Director of Sanitary District, Curriculum Director of Grade

Schools, industry executive, high school teacher involved in school disorder problems). Most children did not mention relationships of a city service or business nature, but cited social activities as routes of acquaintanceship. One child mentioned that the mayor came to a junior league ball game and bought cokes and peanuts for the children; another that he attended the band concerts. One child's parents knew him from the yacht club, another's from church. One father met the mayor when he introduced himself to workers while visiting Abbott Laboratories. Three mentioned spontaneous meetings—on the street, at a restaurant, in a local shop.

These remarks suggest the ways Sabonjian acquires so many "good government" friends. He is doing much more than being simply chief of staff when six to eight times each week he welcomes or addresses conventions, voluntary organizations, and fraternal orders, dedicates church and hospital wings, attends group picnics, dinners, ribbon cuttings, judges contests, serves on innocuous boards, auctions at fund raising events, spends a day at an Ethnic Fellowship Fair chatting with guests from his "mayor's booth," or presenting mayor's trophies. He is meeting, personalizing, and offering assistance to persons who might or might not take him up on it. He is opening the doors through which he may make inroads into the good government forces; he is opening the doors through which he may personalize relationships. Many, many persons preface their office requests with explanations as to where they saw the mayor when he offered to help them with this problem.

There are problems in comparing the following and the good government voters. First is the problem of defining the requests of good government as service and the requests of the following as personal assistance. It is possible to say that the manner and nature of the request is secondary to a large commonality. In each case, constituents are seeking response from their officials to the problems of the here and now—be they jobs, landlords or garbage. At some level, garbage is garbage and it is picked up or it is not. At another level, obtaining a job or public aid may resemble getting leases and building codes enforced or getting one's curbing repaired.

There is also the problem of attributing largely ethnic neighborhood identifications to lower-class neighborhoods and not to middle-class neighborhoods. Although such attachments may be strongest among groups in the regular following, Sabonjian is much concerned also with the word of mouth image he creates in the middle-class neighborhoods. The right kind of image is necessary in reaching for inclusion in the middle-class following those who will self-select, and to arousing the interests or changing the ideas of those who would otherwise not.

It is clear that the rewards for personal assistance and quick service cannot be deduced from a strict exchange economics. One could not cost account. For the politician there are multiple payoffs and multiple costs involved in each act. These are both personal and instrumental.

Probably a small percentage of the mayor's actions are either personally *or* instrumentally costly and rewarding. A few actions might be analytically defined as one or the other but there is overwhelming overlap. Most actions involve both. There are at least two reasons why this is true. The first is the logical convergence of philanthropy or *noblesse oblige* and political expedience. The second is the continuity in relations over time and the politician's awareness of it. Because social networks persist and because social acts are not discrete, it is possible to see the scrambling of personal and instrumental behavior as functional strategy. The executive can do something for completely personal reasons and at the same time know that it is likely that persons he helps today will, if given an opportunity, help him in the future—for equally personal reasons.

Sabonjian is vividly aware of this duplicity in motive and reward. When interviewed, he agreed that his most time-consuming activity is winning electoral support. But he added: "Except it's not just the votes. I enjoy being in a position where I can help people." Sabonjian will only infrequently know the particular political effects of his actions. Particular political effects may only infrequently occur. He can bet, however, on the value of "friendships" he makes out of good will, sympathy, pleasure or interest. He can bet that more often than not he will be paid back for favors extended and that a single person who is grateful will probably bring his positive evaluation to the attention of those close to him. It is not necessary to know whether or not a particular beneficiary ever responds so long as the net effect is positive. While in choice situations some attitudes and some problems may weigh more heavily with the mayor than do others, his normal decision criterion seems to be a general willingness to respond to any low-cost requests which pile up in his office.

There is a final rationale for justifying quick help. The executive can feel that in a fundamental sense he is doing the job he set out to do. He is meeting the needs of his constituents. "I'm here because I want to be here and I'm doing what I'm supposed to be doing." Such political action is consummatory for Sabonjian and probably for other political heads—a value in itself. Mark this reward against cost.

Indifferent Upper Class   The indifferent upper class possess but choose not to exploit politically potent resources. These are the people Dahl says use their money to collect art treasures instead of politicians.[22] The president of the oldest and second largest bank in Waukegan is interested in horses and riding, not in politics. Here is potential but unused power. Indifference to local political activity reaches its peak among this upper resource group. Positions and properties are less threatened by the round of city action, and alternatives in the private sphere are greater. Rather than get mixed up in local politics, it might be simpler to move—change neighborhoods or towns, or move to the country; send one's children to private school, remodel the downtown with private funds, or *buy* the property on the residential through-street where others want to put commercial buildings.

In terms of direct contact, the mayor and this dissociated elite have virtually no business, except insofar as the mayor assumes that these persons, like the good government voters, want safe streets, planted boulevards, clean and progressive government.

Only one occurrence suggested what might distinguish the mayor's indirect relations with these persons. The logic of the mayor's behavior rested precisely on the existence of alternatives such as those I listed above. A developer and friend of the mayor proposed to build a nursing home on the corner of a circular street housing independent, non-political professionals. The conversation went as follows:

Developer: I want to build a really first-class nursing home in Waukegan.

Sabonjian: That's great. Something the city really needs. I'm delighted. Where are you thinking of putting it?

Developer: Right up there on ———————.

Sabonjian: No, you'll have to find another location. The people up there will never stand for it. They want a one family residence area only and it's impossible to talk to them.

Developer: This would be a really Class A place . . .

Sabonjian: Take my word for it. It won't work. I know those people and they're stubborn as hell, absolutely impossible to work with. I'd help you if I could but I just cannot work with that crowd up on ———— (street) and around in there. A few years back somebody came to me about putting a beautiful apartment building on that same site you're looking at. I really wanted this building. We don't yet have anything that nice. And they wouldn't build it unless they could put it there. I gave the permit and you can't imagine the storm. Those residents fought I tell you, and said finally that they'd buy the lot themselves at any price rather than let the building go up. There was nothing to do but withdraw the permit. ———— Motors wanted to put in a car lot five blocks west of ———— (same street) and they did the same thing. There's no chance you'd get the thing built and I'd rather not see you waste your money on estimates. They'd just buy the property out from under you.

While it stands alone, the mayor's statement is intriguing for the distinction it suggests between protesters who can and cannot revert to private means of control. The catch is that a difference in outcome is not as easily discernible. Throughout the city, homeowner protests against multiple dwellings have, with two exceptions, been successful. Sabonjian's awareness of the alternative available to elite groups may have been less important here than the clarity with which he felt he could, on the basis of past experience, predict this neighborhood's response to a nursing home proposal. Given that citizen opposition almost always brings a city retreat, it is conceivable that the mayor would be equally hesitant to make a zoning proposal in any area where he felt opposition was assured.

In concluding this discussion, the reader should be reminded of the scarcity of data on this group. The lack of data is a consequence of several factors. In many cases these persons prefer to use private means in securing ends. Then, too, it is a tiny population that is involved. In Waukegan, high resource persons are not residentially segregated from the much larger population of middle-income families; they are statistically invisible.

In thinking about size, it should be remembered that the "indifferent upper class" corresponds in terms of potential resources to the eighteen persons who were identified as being dominants. The number here is also very small and includes an uninvolved bank president, two inactive owners of local department stores and top executives of industrial plants. Beyond that they are elusive and rare. Unlike the community influentials with whom they share autonomy, these persons are not political actors. Unlike the lower autonomy persons with whom they share constituent status, they are not dependent upon the political order for either livelihood, or personal living standard. Persons with this range of choice have the opportunity to be either localities or cosmopolites. They may well be the latter. Because of their dissociation from local or community life, they are not very interesting as either actors or voters. What importance they have in the eyes of the city's politicians probably lies less in their voting potential than in the slack resources they control.

SUMMARY AND CONCLUSIONS

This chapter began with the proposition that a leader's alternatives are limited by the various pressures he must accommodate if he is to maintain a secure structure of influence. The mayor's "Cage of Pressures" can be described in terms of six categories.

Among participants:

Subleaders include city officials, department heads, campaign workers, and others who work within the network of political/governmental activity to see that the mayor attains the goals he seeks. Their position is usually dependent upon him.

Interest advocates are persons and organized factions which seek to influence government decisions from bases outside the political/governmental arena. They are not dependent upon their association with the political network for primary values, but neither do they have the resources which might be used to exert power over it. They seek personal or organizational goals.

Institutional dominants are also persons or organizations interested in influencing public policy. These leaders possess independent sources of power. The government is one such base: the mayor is one such leader. Successful realization of community goals normally requires cooperation among several of these centers of power.

Among constituents:

The "following" is the corps of loyal voters whose attachment is to the mayor as friend and benefactor rather than as administrator. These voters comprise the mayor's most reliable electoral bloc.

Good government voters are moderately autonomous and largely indifferent. Generally speaking they are proponents of efficient administration, non-controversial city improvements and procedural regularity. On occasion, they can be aroused by specific issues which threaten personal or neighborhood values. They are fickle supporters.

The indifferent upper class are voters who possess potentially powerful political resources but are not oriented to local government as a means of securing ends. They feel neither benefited nor threatened by the actions of local government, preferring to seek goals through alternatives in the private sphere.

Each of these groups is a concern of the executive. Commitments are not equally great, however. The strength of a commitment is determined by its importance to the official's position and his ability to act. The first requisite of political success is electoral victory. In building toward the desirable margins, the politician thinks in terms of two categories of voters—the following and the good government voters. The first group is reliable, the second large.

Office security is greatly enhanced by the creation of a dependable voter following. When party machinery is not available for this purpose (and maybe when it is) the elected official must find other ways to create a following. He must build his own coterie of subleaders and he must gain control over the resources he needs to supply individual benefaction. Since the assistance sought is frequently small in scale, information is often the basis for responsiveness. In providing rewards to the following, Sabonjian capitalized on the resources of everybody in his political contact.

At best, the following is still not likely to provide electoral victory. The executive must work also to acquire support from the more autonomous, issue-oriented, good government voters. If he is to respond to these voters, he must be able to produce in terms of efficient administration and popular public programs. This requires (1) subleader cooperation such that government resources can be mobilized, and (2) the acquisition (from institutional dominants) of power resources beyond those which are strictly governmental (but which are necessary to implementing programs). Thus both subleaders and dominants become vital commitments.

These two components of program success are reciprocals of one another. On the one hand, ability to negotiate with the community leaders requires the politician to be able to secure the compliance of subleaders, to maintain organizational control. Only then can he trade *political* power for economic or other power. The need to negotiate with outside leaders makes more central the politician's commitment to his subleaders. If, on the other hand, the mayor is to establish control over the resources of government, he must be able to reward subleader compliance with appropriate advantage. This requires inputs from outside the governmental sphere as well as control within that sphere. Commitments to other leaders grow stronger. This is particularly true insofar as non-political inputs make it possible for him to dispense private sphere advantages (such as jobs) and realize public sphere programs. The constituent support he gains in these processes can, in turn, secure the positions of his subleaders.

Thus the popularity of Sabonjian and his subleaders grow through the contributions of others—as downtown businessmen remodel and install lighting, contractors donate fountains, industries install lake front lighting, breweries finance ball park trips for retired steelworkers, or industries donate supplies to self-help groups. The following grows as Sabonjian uses community contacts to find jobs for the unemployed, provides legal aid through friends or the city attorney, and finds private financing for the bus lines. Economic interests achieve goals because elected officials are unified and efficient. They benefit when the council takes the necessary actions to retain the courthouse, incorporate the site of the Lakehurst Shopping Mall or bring in a new industry.

The whole system hinges on keeping commitments from coming into conflict—"on working like hell" to achieve goals on which the mayor and other community leaders can agree, on seeing that the resources collected from cooperation here can be turned into advantages for the following and other constituents, on seeing that constituent support can be transferred to subleaders, and on making sure that subleaders will work efficiently on day-to-day organizational maintenance and provide support on those big programs where he sees opportunities for multiple gain.

The next chapters will explore the ways in which the mayor seeks to achieve cooperation and avoid conflict among the various groups to which he is committed.

Note on Typology The analysis in this chapter is based on a single case and Waukegan is a city with a particular distribution of persons along the two variables considered. Because it is a diversified community in socio-economic terms, there is reason to believe the pressures identified in Waukegan have general applicability. In communities which do not share Waukegan's socio-economic distribution, the same pressures would probably be present, though commitments would no doubt vary.

NOTES

[1] Robert Dahl, *Who Governs*, p. 246.

[2] Edward Banfield, *Political Influence*, p. 242.

[3] Scott Greer, *Last Man In* (Free Press, 1959), pp. 75–76.

[4] *Ibid.*, pp. 83–84.

[5] Robert Dahl, "The Analysis of Influence in Local Communities," p. 32; and Chapter IV, *Who Governs*.

[6] Banfield, *Political Influence*, pp. 246–7, 249–50, 256.

[7] Richard Neustadt, *Presidential Power* (Mentor, 1964), Chapter 4.

[8] Melville Dalton, *Men Who Manage* (Wiley, 1969), Chapter 7.

[9] William F. Goode, "The Protection of the Inept," *American Sociological Review* 32 (February, 1967): 15.

[10] Compare to Mayor Daley's remark that: "We all like to hear a man speak out on his convictions and principles. But at the same time, you must remember that when you're running on a ticket, you're running with a team." (Press Conference, *Chicago Daily News*, pp. 2–2768).

[11] Dahl, *supra*, note 5 above.

[12] For the mechanics of list determination see footnote 2, *supra*, Introduction.

[13] The game terminology is borrowed from Norton Long who advises that the local community can best be viewed as an "ecology of games." That is, there is really no overall government in the community, but rather only interaction among a series of activities such as banking, newspaper publishing, contracting, manufacturing, civic organizations, and religious organizations. Interaction takes place among the games because a player must make use of

members of other games in playing his own. Long, "The Local Community as an Ecology of Games."

[14] Dahl, *Who Governs,* p. 151.

[15] *Ibid.,* p. 135.

[16] Banfield, *Political Influence,* p. 229.

[17] *Ibid.,* Chapter 5.

[18] See Dahl's discussion of public sphere recruitment, *Who Governs,* pp. 294–5.

[19] *Chicago Sun Times,* April 12, 1967. In a sense this strategy more accurately describes Sabonjian who gets direct credit from job recipients than it does Daley who must delegate the distribution of jobs and rely on tight control of the distributors for indirect payoff.

[20] V. O. Key, *Southern Politics* (Vintage, 1949), p. 669.

[21] These statements echoed a stand enunciated in a letter to the state highway commissioner early in the highway negotiations. The mayor urged that if the state could move quickly in announcing its plans for property acquisition, "We could set up an orderly plan of relocation for these people. They're entitled to some warning and time for relocation . . . As things stand . . . homeowners on such streets as Kennard, Clinton, May, and Lakeview are hampered in their planning." (5-15-67) In the end the street was rerouted.

[22] Dahl, "The Analysis of Influence in Local Communities," pp. 32–33.

3

Self-Help and Civic Spirit

In a heterogeneous community, the alternatives available to a political head are limited by his commitments to diverse groups. He must maintain equilibrium with groups which are in potential conflict for scarce public resources. Since these groups are functionally interdependent, however, their diversity also constitutes a political resource. Because there is non-integration among interdependent units in the community, a coordinator may produce payoffs formerly not realized and not contradictory. The political coordinator seeks, for action, points in the community where interests are complementary and cooperative networks can be created. Political power is his reward for going beyond, repudiating the zero-sum game.

In the model proposed, he gains power as he (1) facilitates private sphere cooperation among interdependent population segments, "horizontal integration," and (2) uses the power gained in this process to coordinate collective action, "vertical integration." This chapter will deal primarily with "horizontal integration."

INDIVIDUAL CLIENTS

Participant observation drew immediate attention to the range of persons and problems involved in mayoral politics. In his daily office activities, Sabonjian is rarely occupied with programs and issues. On the contrary, by his own estimate, Sabonjian spends some 90 percent of his time assisting people with their "personal problems." In response to Sabonjian's open-door policy, he is flooded with lines of solicitors which frequently stretch out of the office reception room into the hall. To seat this overflow, the hall-way outside the office is lined with chairs. To imagine the variety of requests which reach the mayor's desk would tax the imagination. Yet, the mayor rarely sends away an unsatisfied citizen.

Upon request, he will arrange for one's car repairs, for companions for elderly relatives, for admittance to public housing, for television sets to be sent to hospital patients, for groceries to be delivered to needy families, for books and other items to be shipped to overseas soldiers, for tickets to professional athletic games, for race track passes, and for dinner or motel reservations. He will dispatch the city physician to the homes of indigent families, act upon complaints regarding landlords, credit shysters, garbage pick-up, road repair, tree service, snow plowing, mosquito abatement. He will locate apartments as well as jobs, sell one's house, arrange for boat moorings, provide business or campaign advice, endorse candidates, write college recommendations, issue proclamations dignifying special weeks, and conduct tours for or give talks to any agreeably interested group. Finally, he'll assure anyone whose visiting relatives might be impressed, "Tell them you know the mayor!"

While Sabonjian is amazingly efficient in processing these solicitants, they, nevertheless, by their sheer numbers manage to consume the mayor's day and seemingly to rule out the possibility of any large-scale planning. The city engineer waits hours, sometimes days, to see the mayor while unwed mothers in need of aid and boy scouts wanting to tour, receive almost immediate attention. If, of course, the mayor wanted to see the city engineer and others like him, he could at a moment's notice temporarily or permanently terminate the open-door policy he instead encourages.

The mayor's general assistance policy turns his office into a kind of clearing house. The mayor gets people together and urges cooperation. In facilitating "horizontal integration" in the community he capitalizes on unused resources of influence but does not acquire control over them. There is slack in the use of power resources because in the system as a whole there are ongoing activities which, while they are not themselves political, have a political component. It is not a matter of transferring a resource from non-political to political purposes, but of extracting or siphoning off the political component latent in the normal operation of the "non-political" systems. If an aspirant to power can siphon off the political voltage from transactions which are not primarily political, reaping the political interest for himself, he can build his influence without actually gaining possession of the resources involved.

Take, for example, the distribution of jobs and incomes. There is clearly a political potential latent in this distribution. Yet economic firms do not normally run their hiring policy as a patronage system. Dahl notes that, unlike politicians who use jobs as a potent political weapon, private employers are constrained from doing so. There are various reasons, including "the secret ballot, unionzation, professionalism, and powerful taboos against interfering with their employees' right to vote."[1] Indifference is, no doubt, another factor here.

Nevertheless there is a political potential in the distribution of private as well as public jobs. The fact that this potential is not exploited by those in direct control of the jobs means that there exists an unused political resource. Dahl comments on this potential but does not see it as being important in a system where employers are not politicians and politicians are not employers. He states:

> Some aspects of a community that many citizens would agree were highly important—employment, for example, or the distribution of incomes—lies pretty much beyond the reach of local government. Then, too, in the United States most goods and services are provided by non-governmental rather than governmental agencies.[2]

To the extent that political payoff is not extracted from activities such as the distribution of jobs, there is "slack" in the system of influence.[3] Sabonjian's office activities show how a politician can pick up some of this slack if he so chooses. Sabonjian's tactic is to centralize in himself the influence accompanying such varied control by using the resources he possesses, or over which he has acquired control, to acquire the use of a continually greater range of resources, whether these be jobs, skill, respect, or whatever. He does not gain ownership, it should be noted, but simply superintendence. By making himself the agent through which a variety of resources are distributed, he is able to continually spiral his power and increase his ability to coordinate action. Thus when Sabonjian makes it his business to find jobs in local industries for all those who seek his help, he is the *de facto* distributor of industry jobs and reaps the political profit. The politician who takes this route exploits not only his own resources but the resources of others as well.

There are two ways this situation occurs. One grows out of

indifference on the part of many resource holders. In a very simple sense, Sabonjian does a favor for personnel officers by doing their jobs for them, i.e. he keeps track of job openings and sees that the jobs are filled. It is clear that in many cases personnel officers see the mayor's employment aid as a useful service. A man looking for an office typist called to see if the mayor could help him locate an employee, stating that he was also calling the Illinois Employment Office and other agencies he thought might have applications on file. The personnel director at Fort Sheridan, a nearby army base, informed the mayor by letter that a great many civilian employees were needed at the base, gave the salary range, and requested help from the mayor in locating suitable employees. Many small business proprietors find part-time student help through the mayor's office.

A second way in which the mayor gains distributive prerogative over the resources of others is through actual exchanges with owners of resources. The political head may use his control over certain constitutional functions or control of the council to buy the use of economic resources e.g. by facilitating zoning changes desired by the industrialist for the opportunity to dispense jobs in his factory. During most of the year personnel officials seem happy enough to have jobs filled, but in his search for 450 summer jobs for youth, the mayor often presses their capacity. Pleas begin to go to company presidents as well as personnel officials and Sabonjian sees clearly that it is now a question of favors and an appeal to civic spirit. When a policeman asked Sabonjian's help in acquiring low numbered license plates for his car, Sabonjian said he couldn't help: "Mine aren't even low. I had 101 but I got it transferred to ————— (president of a local industry). I had to. He's been great about hiring kids for me."

The summer job problem is apparently a strain on the Daley administration as well. An ex-member of his staff says it almost goes without question that businesses, industries, and others seeking help from the mayor will be expected to contribute a reasonable number of jobs to "Mayor Daley's Summer Jobs for Youth." To the degree that exchanges like this provide advantages to those who allow their mayor to distribute their resources (and they do), the gain is likely to be greater, proportionate to cost, and certainly more direct, than would be the gain extracted through the use of jobs or other favors to control votes and thereby influence political decisions. The second process is tedious, requires much greater effort, and produces less reliable results.

The mayor has two types of private-sphere job programs: 1) costless—as when both employers and employee benefit from the mayor's distribution; and 2) with some cost—as in the cases where the mayor acquires some indebtedness to employers for the opportunity to distribute jobs. Between these two types of programs, the mayor spends enormous amounts of time in the job business. During the two week period when youths begin their search for summer jobs and 450 are found, the mayor's time for other business is almost totally preempted. During the remaining year, also, the hiring hall remains time-consuming. Forty percent of those on the mayor's list of "frequently called numbers" were phone numbers of personnel officials.

Job distribution of either of these types is a part of a more general strategy of resource distribution. A large inventory of influence is built, as the mayor performs a multitude of personal favors, which draw many varied interests into his debt. He continually has more resources within his control which he may use to answer needs which will, in turn, secure him new debtors and new resources. "Glad to help you," Sabonjian said after managing one such favor. "Now there's something you can do for me. I have a friend who needs —————. I help you. You help my friends. That's the way we all work together." The man for whom Sabonjian finds an apartment today may be able to supply Sabonjian tomorrow with the hockey tickets he wants in order to fill another request.

Such reciprocity, however, is not normally formalized. Although in phrases such as "He owes me a favor," specific reciprocities are implied, others such as "He's been so darned good to me" or "I work real good with —————" suggest a general build-up of non-specific reciprocity. The process snowballs.

Thus, over time, the mayor becomes a job patron, a real estate agent, a medical service, an entertainment bureau, a high status friend, an instructor in politics, and economic advisor. With each transaction, he increases his influence. He is able to supply this range of favors because he has performed other favors and, in most cases, someone who "owes him a favor" has the resource necessary to respond to a new request—whatever it might be.

In ideal form this model would imply that regardless of the

nature of the desire, the political executive would be the channel through which it is obtained. One comic incident suggests that, with regard to the hiring hall run out of the Mayor's office, this point has nearly been reached. It occurred during peak season for job hunters—that period when college students seeking summer jobs join the ranks of the unemployed. Persons who obtain their jobs through the mayor leave with a note from him to the head of personnel at the particular industry. In a single week, dozens of these letters had been sent to the personnel department of a box factory in neighboring North Chicago. When a young man on his own initiative appeared at the factory's personnel office looking for a job, he was sent to get a letter from the mayor of Waukegan. It seems, given that he was the first job applicant to appear in a several week period without such a letter, a new personnel officer had assumed that the letter was standard procedure.

The story illustrates the degree to which the operations in the mayor's office had undercut what is assumed to be normal procedure for distributing jobs—i.e. applicants approach employment offices or personnel officials who distribute jobs among those applying. The fact that there is so much slippage in the operation of the "normal" system provides an enterprising politician with a resource of influence. The mayor capitalizes on the fact that the society itself is not more integrated; that, for example, the communications between employers and potential employees is not more satisfactory; more generally, that many persons do not know how to obtain the things they need or desire—at least not as efficiently as the mayor can do it for them.

GROUPS AND INSTITUTIONS

One should not assume that the mayor's integrative role is limited to the dispensation of personal assistance. When cooperation among others will pull segments of the community together and on the side produce a payoff for Sabonjian and the incumbent politicians, the mayor is quick to offer his services as an idea-man, middleman, cheerleader, and sponsor.

Programs for economic and physical development of the city (such as city beautification or a high employment rate)—whether private or public in origin—constitute capital investments for those charged with the care of the city's physical plant and the socio-economic welfare of its citizens. In many cases, however, the costs to the political order of achieving such goals appear to exceed the gains they would afford. While the executive might desire proposed changes, he does not want to undertake personal direction of programs. Nevertheless, the political structure can *participate* in the realization of goals without eliciting the attention it might if trying to direct action toward them.

During the period of this study's coverage, Sabonjian undertook personal coordination of action toward specific ends on rare occasions only. The only three programs he adopted as personal goals were the city beautification program, the shopping mall, and the civic center. With regard to these programs, he assumed the position of director, insisted upon compliance, called in debts, used up resources, and bet on big winnings. Far more frequent than personal direction was his support for programs which involved smaller cost to himself even if this meant, as in the case of the personal favors, that gains were small and indirect. Sabonjian was a constant booster and a useful friend for those private sector programs which promised indirect, low cost payoff.

His strategy with regard to private real estate development is illustrative. The Waukegan *News-Sun* reports that in an address to the Lake County Contractors Association:

> Mayor Sabonjian challenged contractors to participate in the growth of Waukegan, which he said is reaching for the sky in apartment development. . . . Mayor Sabonjian bluntly challenged the contractors to look into the possibility of development of high-rise apartment buildings. . . . (6-28-68)

The contribution of such projects to the physical growth and renovation of the city would, of course, reflect on but not be costly to the current administration. In addition, real estate development would provide more jobs and lucrative contracts for Waukegan building industries. Sabonjian does not overlook the political potential in these gains, but works actively to see that they in fact occur and that he reaps the political payoff. Toward this end, city contracts go to those contractors who will agree to hire only Waukegan workers (to the political advantage of local unions and the mayor's hiring hall) and to use only Waukegan products when they are available. The lucky recipients of these deals (producers and unions) learn quickly of the source of their benefaction. In addition, municipal officials can use their control over licenses, building permits, zoning regulations and inspection policies to get the same results from non-city contracting and to be sure that bargains are upheld. More or less punitive inspection policies, for example, may be exchanged for in-city purchasing and in-city employment. Such tactics may be implied in the following statement.

> The mayor reiterated his support of Lake County Contractors as long as they support the Waukegan trade unions and purchase their materials in the area. (6-28-68)

More specific suggestions of reward lie behind such public statements as the following.

> We have to do something about middle-income housing. . . . We're not ready for the influx of people that we must have for . . . new industries. The city is willing to work with developers in making more housing available . . . [but] we're going to have to sit down, as people, chambers of commerce, industrial people, and assist the city officials in a proper program—give us ideas on how many employees you expect over the next two years, so we can be prepared to make such changes in our building codes, our zoning, and our planning. (10-12-67)

Here Mayor Sabonjian while insisting that most housing remain in the private sector, states his preferences, offers his services as coordinator. He suggests ways in which the city, through adopting building codes and zoning, can provide advantages to developers interested in cooperating with him in the realization of mutual goals, in this case middle-income housing.

In a similar statement, Sabonjian proposed a plan to work with businessmen in spurring downtown business. He offered to close off the main street at specified times in order to create a mall effect, but demanded cooperation from those who would gain, and refused to undertake the project in the absence of that cooperation.

> Sabonjian said the success of the plan will hinge on the cooperation of the merchants in opening their off-street parking lots and in picking up the cost of Genesee Street parking meters. . . . (7-16-68)

The proposal for action is not necessarily progressive nor preventive. It may be remedial as in the cases where, because of financial losses to the firms running bus and ambulance services, the city faced first the loss of its bus service and later the loss of ambulance service. Sabonjian's responses to these crises were consistent.

When the bus company threatened to abandon its operation, the mayor sought to find a solution which would assure continuation of service without requiring municipal ownership of bus lines. It could be accomplished, he felt, through aid from private organizations which he was willing to organize, encourage and assist. He turned to those in the community who benefit from bus service.

> Sabonjian said he will seek a meeting with other municipalities, the Chamber of Commerce, and businesses to discuss aiding the company at a rate of $2500 a month.
>
> He proposed a fare increase to 30 cents, a nickel more than at present. . . .
>
> The mayor said the bus drivers' union is going along with the attempt to keep the lines open by agreeing to work under the terms of the existing contract. . . . (10-18-68)

When the industry and business leaders who saw advantage in subsidizing the lines sought an audit of the bus company's books to evaluate the necessity of the subsidy, Sabonjian "authorized the city's auditing team . . . to make a review of the books" (10-21-68). He not only provided free auditing services to organizations cooperating in the subsidy but insisted that the municipalities of Waukegan, North Chicago, and Zion could come up with about one thousand dollars a month (10-21-68).

Finally,

> The mayor . . . requested tax supported groups and other organizations to charter buses from Waukegan-North Chicago Transit Company for their trips. (10-21-68)

Sabonjian's program was not for municipal direction or support but for cooperation among all those who would gain from bus line continuation—employers, bus-users, bus-drivers, the bus company management, the city and private organizations. Agreement on a multiple group subsidy was announced January 22, 1969.

Sabonjian's strategy of self-help with city assistance is not limited by audience. For example:

> Mayor Robert Sabonjian came out strong Monday night for more recreational facilities on the south side. But he said that neighborhood adults have to pitch in and help. . . . Sabonjian said school gyms could be made available if adequate supervision can be found.

. . . "But I'm not going to do and ask people to do, if some of the parents won't cooperate, and if some of the leaders won't cooperate." (9-23-68)

When others are willing to participate, Sabonjian is enthusiastic and scrupulously honest with regard to fulfilling his offers of assistance.

> Residents of Waukegan's south side have begun an ambitious clean-up and recreational program that could greatly benefit the entire community. The project has the cooperation of the city administration which has committed itself to aid in any way possible. . . . "They said they had this project in mind and wanted the cooperation of the city," Sabonjian said. "We were happy to give it and will do everything possible to aid them.". . . Sabonjian told the group that use of school buildings was possible—if adult supervision is forthcoming from the community. . . . (8-8-67)

Sabonjian arranged space for a tot lot in connection with the proposed recreation program, cleared a nearby junk yard and provided play equipment (8-8-67).

> In a similar action:
> Mayor Sabonjian today endorsed the ideal of an employment service for teenagers—a proposal of the Lake County Community Action Project. Sabonjian said he will attempt to find office space which would be donated for the summer time project. (6-67)

Such space Sabonjian would hope to obtain not as a favor to himself but from an organization independently interested in the project or he would hope to interest an organization in the public relations potential of the gesture. In such cases, the mayor has no cost and double gain. By capitalizing on communications centrality and slippage in the system, he avoids "paying" for profitable action.

The possibility of low cost gain was available in innumerable other instances. In the building of the half-way house, Sabonjian arranged for the building to be painted by the local contractor's association. In the case of the Becker House, a home established to provide a transition for youths from institutional to community life, he assisted with zoning needs, located a director and made arrangements for furnishing the building. When the Illinois Home and Aid Society sponsored a charity luncheon, Sabonjian arranged for the food to be donated by various restaurants and stores, for the gas company to donate the building, and for a local restaurant to loan the group its chef. He arranged for furniture, a station wagon, and a playground to be obtained by a black nursery school—in addition to raising funds. He initiated a program whereby persons who would purchase trees for their yards could have them planted by the city without cost. When a local hospital decided to participate in a federal program whereby medical supplies for use in disasters would be stockpiled at the hospital, the mayor found a local van company which would donate the use of a van to bring the emergency equipment into the city and he offered the services of city employees to do the actual moving of the supplies. To facilitate the participation of the Lake County Contractors Association in a federally financed program to train cement masons, Sabonjian made city property available for classroom space. When a civic group decided to paint the beach concession stand, he arranged for local paint shops to donate the paint. When a group of Mexican-Americans offered to fix up a neighborhood park, Sabonjian arranged for donations of paint, equipment, and the necessary lighting. When the girl scouts remodeled, Sabonjian was responsible for the donation and installation of air conditioners. When high school groups hold car washes, Sabonjian provides soap and towels and has all the city vehicles washed—"so they'll know we're with them."

In private session with leaders of the NAACP, Sabonjian made a proposal which is typical of those which produce these kinds of projects.

> If you can find people who will paint their house, I'll go down to ———— (Waukegan paint factory) and get them to donate however much paint it will take to get every home in the ghetto painted. If they'll paint the inside, I'll see that they get new furniture to put in it. I'll go to ————, and the rest of the furniture stores that don't normally take trade-ins, tell them to take in the old stuff when they sell new, then get them to donate it. I'll get your appliances donated. All I need is people to help me, so I can sell the idea. . . . Look what I've been able to do for the Puerto Ricans with Eddy to help me.

Sabonjian is furious with those who will not cooperate with him in achieving those goals which he feels point toward a bigger, better Waukegan. He has harsh words for opposition aldermen in personal letters sent from the mayor to every home in the alderman's ward. Other non-cooperation is similarly attacked.

The mayor, who has been finding jobs for needy youngsters for many years, said that he was disappointed this year by the lack of interest on the part of area businessmen.

He pointed out that these youngsters are willing to work and need the money to return to college in the fall.

"They maintain that a youngster has to be 18 before he can be employed because of insurance. I am sure they can find a loophole in that."

The Mayor said that one industry in the area—which he did not name—could not come up with even one job. ". . . I don't believe them."

"It is time that industry opened its doors to the kids of our community," he said. "They expect our kids to grow up to be good citizens. They have to have a break."

The mayor said there are plenty of stores in the area that could use extra clerks and stockboys.

"They use these youngsters during school hours. If they can do it then they can do it during the summer.

"I am asking publicly that we have a barrage of jobs available for these ambitious young citizens of our community who are seeking to get ahead by continuing their education."

The mayor pointed out that the city, itself, hires about 100 youngsters every summer to aid them in their search for improvement. (6-10-69)

Sabonjian never accepts a "no" and as the jobs, in fact, run out, his moral indignation over this lack of community interest grows. "I can't do it by myself. You've got to help. Find some jobs, Make them."

Black groups who won't cooperate get the same treatment.

"We think it is about time that some of the concerned black citizens do something on their own for youngsters before they get into trouble with the police," Sabonjian said.

He pointed out that he had opened the gymnasiums of the city for the children to play in and could not get anyone from the black community to supervise the program. (9-11-69)

"And the Negroes who serve on committees," he contended, "are accused by some of their own people as being Uncle Toms . . .

"The city can't do it all. You are the city. The people have to do something." (3-13-69)

Directing his fury to area industries who refused to enter floats in the city's Christmas parade he said:

"Every industry in Waukegan and North Chicago flatly refused. I heard from one or two fellows, pretty reliable sources, that possibly the reason why, that just about this time of the year, some of these junior executives, or whatever you want to call them, I guess they get a bonus if they operate below their budget, so I guess they don't want to put out the money.

—"This town has been good to industry. I think we've been very, very good to industry. . . .

"I think we should quit dividing dollars and cents against civic obligation, civic participation. I think there should be no line between obligation and loyalty to the place where you have your business and make your living—and where the people who work for you live.

"I say this to the leaders of all segments of society, the sooner people realize their obligations and assume their own responsibilities —there will be less use and need for these so-called wailing walls and commissions on this and commissions on that and commissions on everything else." (11-22-67)

When cooperation is seen as essential, there are usually means to require it. The punitive use of legal prerogative in order to obtain compliance is expressed in a story told about Mayor Daley by an informed Chicago attorney. It is illegal, he says, for the mayor to order bars in areas of civil disorder to close until order is restored. An order to close a bar can be issued only after a formal hearing, for which a two-week advance notice is required. Thus Daley issues formal requests that bars cooperate with the city in closing until calm is restored. The informal message which accompanies such requests is that failure to cooperate will result in a hearing where some violation will be found and the bar's license revoked.

When, on the other hand, groups propose or accept Sabonjian's appeal to cooperate and invest resources in city projects, he is laudatory as well as helpful.

"The important responsibility St. Therese Hospital assumed to take care of Waukegan and Lake County residents in case of disaster is typical of the hospital's outstanding record of community service," Sabonjian said.

"I know the hospital can count on continued whole-hearted support and I hope all others concerned with health, Civil Defense, and community service will work with St. Therese to make sure it will have the most effective packaged disaster plan in the state." (6-67)

Other evidences of civic spirit are rewarded too:
In a personal letter—

Dear Mrs. —————:
   I certainly appreciate your interest in our bus company problems for Waukegan. The article you sent to me is very interesting and I am using it in my studies of what to do to keep our busses running.
   It thrills me to know that I have citizens who sincerely try to help our city and take the time to offer constructive suggestions.

In public statements—

Sabonjian said he was glad to see company executives deciding to live in Waukegan instead of settling in the fashionable [Chicago] suburbs to the south. (1-22-69)
   Mayor Robert Sabonjian helped kick-off a League of Women Voters of Waukegan finance drive Monday by praising the league's efforts on a recently published history of Waukegan. (8-6-68)

(In addition to praising the League's research, Sabonjian helped out some by providing city financing for the actual printing and hardback publication of the book and for its free distribution to schools, the library, and public offices.)
   Sabonjian greatly admires John F. Kennedy whom he sees as spokesman for the integrative ideal. Indeed, all of the portraits (three) in his private office are of JFK and/or his family and another picture of the Kennedys greets visitors in the reception room. He has a large plaque (which he shows frequently and with great pride) where Kennedy's famous "Ask not what your country can do for you, but what you can do for your country" is inscribed. Seeing Waukegan as a microcosm he takes the lead: "As your mayor I pledge myself to make this a wonderful community for everyone but everyone must carry their load of the bargain too" (11-22-67).
   What might be comic in this identification is transformed when one understands the mayor's tactical understanding of his role. I asked him how he changed what had been a weak mayor town under his predecessor into the centralized order it is today:

The powers were there when Coulson was in office just the same as

they are now. He just didn't seize them on account of his interpretation of the constitution. When they asked him about his position,
he always said "We have a weak mayor town—a strong council
town." I say, "We work together."

More specifically:

You seize the power where it is. You use your appointive powers
so as to make working together profitable and use your contracts
and whatever else you've got for the same thing. Then it pays off
for everybody to work together and the thing grows.

And when it grows, Sabonjian does get credit—credit which is
indirect but real. A pre-election *News-Sun* editorial stated that:

He has earned that type of voter support by his efforts in behalf
of youth activities, street improvements, industrial and business
expansion and the maintenance of police and fire protection. And
he has often used the power of persuasion, rather than the public
pocketbook, to achieve progress.

There are various other bonuses for the politician who can organize the achievement of goals in this way. Helping those who
help themselves allows him universalistic standards for the dispensation of particularistic rewards. And it produces something
like dollar-matching from those who seek change—thus multiply-
ing output for relative city input.

Also, since rewards go to those self-movers who seek to cooperate
with one another and with the city—those who accept its goals
and its unity—it allows the mayor, by using what are the true
gains of cooperative action, to control cleavage and opposition. By
encouraging organized groups (as well as private persons) to
channel problems through his office and producing benefits for
those who do, he coopts ever more participants into his personal
sphere of influence. When I asked Sabonjian whether he found
his job easier or harder than when he took office, he said:

Oh, easier. I've got more friends. This may sound corny, but I'm
in a better position to help people. I can get things done better now
because I know more people. I've got more contacts, more avenues
of information. You know, I've got more people I can call on for
help. And, I don't want you to get this wrong, but I've got more
ways to exert pressure on people I couldn't have pressured before.

As an executive extends his own access to resources and his personal ability to respond, he undercuts the ability of opposition to recruit support.[4] It becomes increasingly difficult for others to produce similar rewards and opposition can cause one to lose advantages he had. This is clear in the following conversation between Sabonjian and a group of dissident Puerto Ricans who were seeking Sabonjian's support for a Puerto Rican aldermanic candidate who was running without the support of the established Puerto Rican leader.

Puerto Rican spokesman: "Before we go, I'd like to make it clear that you don't need to worry about ——— if he is elected. He's been for you all along."

Sabonjian: "He'd better be for me. All I'd need to do would be to not give any jobs to Puerto Ricans for six months and the Puerto Ricans would lynch him. How do you think alderman M—— and A—— got beat in the primary? Every time somebody in their ward called me up to complain, I told them to call their other alderman, because I couldn't work with M—— or A——"

Using his appointees, his contacts, and his friends to reward and withhold, Sabonjian saw defeated his only two aldermanic opponents in the 1967 election. In 1969, every aldermanic candidate (Democratic and Republican alike) endorsed Sabonjian for mayor.

However, Sabonjian prefers to avoid punitive control. When asked if he didn't spend more time with the problems of his subleaders than with those of the reputed influentials, he replied:

> Oh yes. I romance my aldermen. You remember when I cut those three guys off . . . when I stripped them of all committees and asked people not to vote for them. And the News-Sun headlines were "Mayor cuts 3 GOP aldermen from Council Committees." That's not the way I like it at all. But those guys opposed everything—on general principle. So I said, "All right, you three can just be a committee of three opposed to everything." But for the most part we work together. But that's leadership, not dictatorship. You do something for them; they return the favor. And you all get elected because by working together you're able to do a job.

Sabonjian tries to apply this strategy to leadership throughout the community, hoping that those leaders who cooperate with the city will be able to produce most effectively for their groups and thereby to lead most effectively. For years Sabonjian and the president of NAACP have been at odds. When a delegation of NAACP members showed up without this man, Sabonjian bent over backwards to see that they would be satisfied with the outcome of the meeting, declaring throughout the meeting how happy he was to see them and how fortunate it was that *they* could work together. While he did not appoint to the school board the particular person whose appointment they sought, he agreed to appoint two black members instead of the one he had originally planned. In addition, he made offer after offer for programs which he hoped they might undertake jointly—among them plans for a summer camp and for renovation of south side homes.

After a policy settlement had been reached with the NAACP group, Sabonjian turned to the individual member who had sought appointment and proposed that he should be appointed to the Planning Commission. When the man hesitated, Sabonjian continued, "If you're interested in city problems, I *insist* upon giving you a chance to contribute."

Insofar as a political executive is successful in establishing close communication with the effective leaders of the various groups in the community, he increases his ability to receive early consultation. He is able to suggest and persuade and he gains the opportunity to negotiate early, non-divisive compromises.

His irritation with the Puerto Rican aldermanic candidate was a result of the candidate's refusing to allow him this advantage. He told the group who had come in the candidate's behalf:

> So all of the sudden I get word that ——— has his petitions out. Then he comes in here and asks me if I want him to withdraw. "You just say the word, Mayor, and I'll drop out," he says. Nobody came to me before you decided to run a Puerto Rican candidate. Then after his petitions were out, he asks me if I want him to withdraw. I couldn't have him withdraw then without embarrassing myself. I'd have looked like a dictator. If he would have come to me first, I would have told him to wait awhile and we'd run him next time. Even so, I told him: "Look, I've got to stick with [incumbent] but I'll try to get you on Cepon's ticket." [County office] Twice I took him by the hand down to Cepon's office and tried to get him on Cepon's ticket.

Similarly, Sabonjian was enraged when he heard secondhand of the threatened bus pull out. He told representatives of the bus driver's union that the company president "should have talked it over with me. Tell those guys that before they go to the commerce commission, they should at least talk to me." When trouble is not averted in this way, Sabonjian sets his sights on the next round. "Next time, see me *first*." "Somebody should have talked to us." "Check with me before you do something like this again. I could have told you it wouldn't work." In interviews, each of Waukegan's top eighteen reputational influentials asserted that his first step in realizing a project would be to clear it with the mayor, whose approval would be critical.

It is at this point that the integrative and directive roles of the mayor merge and overlap. In selecting the projects he will assist and producing compromises where he cannot accept, the mayor becomes director of what Homans calls the "moving equilibrium." The integrative component becomes a prerequisite for directive action. The executive's offer of assistance—an offer to facilitate cooperation—presumes a cooperative potential and a cooperative intent.

This constitutes direction insofar as it reduces the likelihood that special interest proposals will be achieved or radical change effected. It maximizes the opportunities for small projects (those which do not require cooperation from too many segments in the community) and for non-controversial action. It assists efforts to extend and to elaborate but not to oppose. It allows those changes which can be instituted without serious threat to the consensus in the community. Under the mayor's supervision, the equilibrium "moves" but does not leap.

There is further support for these conclusions through examination of what appeared at first to be deviant cases. Over the period of this study, Sabonjian rarely failed to be a public booster to self-help groups. Those cases where he was not can be explained without damage to this theory. Sabonjian endorsed but clearly did not sponsor what turned out to be a successful campaign to pass a county junior college referendum. That is, while publicly urging its passage, he sent no personal letters or vote canvassers. He did not appear in its behalf or advise campaign organizers. He applied no pressure, called in no debts. He explained his virtual abstention:

I was for it all right, but it wasn't something for just Waukegan and in this case I was afraid I'd do more harm than good. There was a lot of resentment in the county when I fought to get the court-house located here. I thought it might really divide the county if I pushed for the Junior College. They'd think that meant I intended to get it for Waukegan, too. Outside Waukegan there'd be a lot of people saying, "There goes Sabonjian again trying to get everything for Waukegan." I felt in this case I could help more by abstaining. Also, I helped by dropping my drive for a vocational school. When I pulled back on that it gave the junior college a better chance.

Other cases where the mayor's absence as a cooperative agent was conspicuous can be discussed in terms of two categories. Both categories are defined by their cleavage-producing characteristics. These two categories are: (1) Proposals made by groups which are distinguished by a cleavage ideology; and (2) Proposals characterized by a high controversy potential.

Groups in the first category are by definition uncooperative. Cooperation with the city is "selling out." Those who compromise are "cop-outs" and "Uncle Toms." Groups characterized by ideological separation range from those which subscribe to simple dissociation to those which engage in active opposition. The mayor responds accordingly.

A black youth group began a series of presumably constructive programs in the south side ghetto—teen socials, field trips, art workshops, a lecture series, and drama and music clinics. Sabonjian explained why he had not helped in any of these programs: "I tried. I did everything I could to horn in. I made offer after offer after offer. But they don't want help. They want to do it themselves." While he has no reason to be hostile or take action *against* these groups, their insistence upon exclusiveness denies him many of the opportunities for gain which have been discussed in this chapter. Thus, he continues to help those groups which seek his help and refuses for the most part to recognize the segregationist groups. Stating at a council meeting that he was opposed to the federal poverty program (which bypassed city government) he was asked "Could your opposition be because you are not involved?" Sabonjian replied, "You are probably right" (3-13-69). On the other hand, Sabonjian does not fail to see gains when they occur and to recognize the value in administrative association with them. Thus, in spite of its exclusiveness, he gave "Head Start" a weak endorsement.

When groups propose action which is not simply exclusive of

but in opposition to community unity, the city chief is apt to escalate his opposition. The legality, for example, which Dahl discusses for its ability to reward can also be used to control. Underworld gang leaders in major American cities have gone to prison on income tax evasion; members of street gangs and the leaders in riots have been busted for narcotics. In Waukegan, a faction of the Students for Democratic Society ran into this kind of opposition from the city when they began what they called the "Waukegan Movement." The prime targets of the "Waukegan Movement" were the draft, the police, and the "dictatorship" of "Rock" Sabonjian. While engaged in their assault on authority (which in its early stages was feared by city officials as organized subversion) SDS members found themselves arrested for a variety of legal offenses including the posting of handbills on private property, disorderly conduct, possession of pornographic literature, and assaulting a patrolman. When, following an FBI investigation, the mayor decided that the SDS threat was not serious, he reverted to the strategy he uses in combating "legitimate" non-structural opposition (such as that from opposition candidates). He ignored the Movement, denied it the publicity his opposition would afford, and continued to assist cooperative groups.

Between groups which dissociate and groups which oppose are groups which act as critics of the prevailing integration. While this constitutes pretty low level opposition, it is somewhat more serious than simple exclusion (albeit less serious than organizational opposition). In the end, the Waukegan Movement was classified in this way. A variation on the notion of ideological opposition is generalized opposition, as in the case of the three aldermen who in the mayor's view "opposed everything." Finally this classification includes groups which, while purporting to seek cooperative action, select goals which the mayor feels are impossible to achieve in the local community. When groups or factions ask what seems technically impossible to achieve, it is read as an indication that such groups are not really interested in cooperating with the city but in criticizing it. At any rate, they become effective critics since the administration's response is inevitably inadequate. Sabonjian sees his major problems as mayor in the following terms:

These people who make a big fuss about . . . problems which are too big for solutions—and anyhow they don't want solutions. They just want to criticize. Take ————. All he wants to do is talk about whose fault the Negro situation is. "Whose fault in the first place?" all the time. So O.K., it's ours. But let's forget the past. What can we do about it NOW?

When a representative of the state human relations office came to discuss better communications with the black community, the mayor became angry:

I had this mayor's commission on human relations. But there wasn't anybody to talk to. No leader representing. We used to have rapport with the Negro leaders. Now the older leaders are called "Uncle Toms." But there aren't any new leaders to replace them. The new guys don't want to talk about problems in the community. All they want to talk about is white supremacy and the Viet Nam war,—things I can't do anything about.

When in this same conversation, the state representative accused the council of being hostile to the demands of black citizens, Sabonjian defended the council:

The council is very open. A Negro man came the other night about sewer improvement. An old guy. He came like a gentleman with a legitimate request, and the council moved to help. When somebody comes in with a chip on his shoulder and starts yelling and accusing, naturally they start yelling back.

The second category of proposal where the mayor's cooperation was conspicuously absent is related to the problem of the impossible proposal. In this case, however, it is not the belligerence or insincerity of the group proposing which frustrates action, but the nature of the proposal. While the plan set forth may be technically possible to achieve and sincerely sought, it is, in the politician's view, politically impossible. It was the mayor's reading of the political context which frustrated the sincerely cooperative intent of the groups which proposed urban renewal, and the one-way street.

In Waukegan, both differentiation and interdependence are givens. What follows in terms of cleavage or integration is not. For an incumbent politician with the whole as his constituency, it must be integration. Voter dependence and constituent heterogeneity combine to make the integrative strategy the only strategy which is politically sound. Through frenetic personal effort, Sabonjian seeks the values of integration to be realized and opposition, in turn, made impractical.

Yet, the integrative strategy can be supported by a highly defensible morality. The moral concomitant to electoral reality becomes "I am mayor of this city—all of it. I am mayor of the people—all of them." As Mayor Sabonjian said when he switched party labels, "I've always thought city politics should be on a nonpartisan level and my first responsibility is to the people" (1-10-69). Or as Mayor Daley said in his 1955 inaugural address:

> I ran as a Democratic candidate for mayor of Chicago. I am proud to be a Democrat. Tonight, however, as Mayor of Chicago—I want to declare for all to hear—that my employer is all the people of Chicago—Democrats, Republicans, and Independents—of every economic group, of every neighborhood and every community.[5]

The mayor accounts costs both practically and morally in terms of what action will do to the consensus of the community.

NOTES

[1] Dahl, *Who Governs*, p. 250.

[2] *Ibid.*, pp. 219–220.

[3] This proposition is an extension of Dahl's notion of "slack" in the system of influence. He defines slack as the existence of "unused and inefficiently used resources of influence." Dahl, "The Analysis of Influence in Local Communities," 35. According to Dahl, a political entrepreneur pyramids his power by picking up slack — by obtaining new (unused) resources, or by better exploiting those he has. See also, Chapter V, *Who Governs*.

[4] Jiri Kolaja notes that an important consequence of including workers in the management of Yugoslav factories was to undercut the power of unions by providing personal access to officials, thus inside channels for grievance. He found that while the inexperienced workers hesitated to challenge the management policies of hired administrators, they did take advantage of their new inside status to seek personal rather than group redress of grievances. Kolaja, *Workers Councils* (Praeger, 1966).

[5] Inaugural address, April 20, 1955.

4

Setting the Civic Agenda

While horizontal integration accords a certain indirect and subtle control to the mayor, there are occasions when political organization is mobilized toward specific public sphere goals. As the political leader facilitates the ability of groups to achieve private sphere goals, he acquires power which can be used for central direction.

Peter Blau discusses the ability of a powerful person to achieve further power through vertical coordination of a collective.

> An individual who has power over an entire group can coordinate their activities in the pursuit of various ends by telling them each what to do. By giving orders to others and imposing his will upon them, the ruler or leader cashes in on some of the obligations they owe him for whatever services and thus depletes his power. . . . But, if the coordination is effective, it furthers the achievement of some goals, that is, it brings rewards that would not have been obtained otherwise. . . In these cases the benefit group members derive due to the leader's effectiveness more than replenish his credit and their obligations to him, which were partly used up by their compliance with his directives. . . . The leader can distribute some of the extra benefits resulting from his contribution to his subordinates and still maintain a surplus for himself, increasing his power over subordinates while making special profits besides.[1]

Blau indicates that coordination of collective action is a means by which a political head secures his position as leader. Yet, the initial effect of such coordination is receipt of accumulated obligations and consequent depletion of power. If successful, the risk is rewarded with increased profits. If unsuccessful, the result is depletion of power and threat to position.

Talcott Parsons formulates this problem with specific regard to politicians and constituents. He compares a system of influence to credit banking. Parsons notes that "an operating bank is in 'one' important sense always formally 'insolvent,' in that its deposits are held on demand whereas its loans are on term." The elected politician is like the bank. He may invest power allocated to (invested with) him in "collective enterprises that are not direct responses to the interest-demands of constituents." However,

> if the electorate, like the bank's depositors, should demand immediate and strict accounting of power, the system would, like a good bank, turn out to be "insolvent" in the sense that these commitments could not be liquidated all at once. Often, however, the politicians can shrewdly estimate the latitude it is safe to assume in making commitments other than those specifically demanded by the constituents on whom they are dependent.[2]

Since he must at frequent intervals appear "solvent," the political head must select carefully the issues he will support and those he will spearhead. Those which bring his commitments into conflict, he will want to suppress. It is to the advantage of the political head to control the scale, timing and definition of issues. If these things are determined by persons concerned with a different set of commitments than his own, or by general controversy, it is possible that the outcome will not be optimal from his point of view.

THE POLITICAL TIMETABLE

With regard to several issues Sabonjian assumed aggressive leadership; with regard to others he was disinterested (and because aggressive action was required, disinterest was tantamount to opposition). The question of "solvency" was critical to his decision to act or to avoid action.

An issue of the first sort was the incorporation and construction of the Lakehurst shopping and residential complex. Locating the one hundred million dollar development in Waukegan required the coordination of multiple groups. The developers' proposed site was an unincorporated area located a short distance west of Waukegan, separated from the city by a small municipality known as Park City. Since some $750,000 annual sales tax revenue was expected, there arose considerable dispute as to what political jurisdiction would claim the development. Bringing it eventually to Waukegan required the cooperation of the city with developers and leader stores (Carson, Pirie, Scott, and Co., Wieboldt's, J. C. Penney). It required the cooperation of political entities which were original competitors for the shopping mall. Necessary roadways could be supplied only with the cooperation of the Lake County and Illinois State Highway Commissions. Annexing the property required also a corridor through Park City. Property owners in the area had to be induced to petition for annexation to Waukegan. A school district plan capable of handling the expected school influx had to be agreed upon. Unless all these contingencies could be worked out, legal passage would have been meaningless. Because the mayor's past centralization of government resources was sufficient to secure council passage of the annexation proposal and to assure financial allocations for roads, sewers, and water, he had a strong hand in negotiations with county, state and business interests. Once he had the necessary commitments from the council, the mayor could offer water lines from Waukegan to land-locked Park City in exchange for the needed corridor. With commitments from major stores, he could induce additional stores to locate. With incorporation and amenities assured and businesses committed to the arrangement, he could defeat county hopes for the complex and negotiate with county officials for assistance in necessary road building.

The $2.8 million civic center which the mayor has proposed for Waukegan is another example of this process. Discussion began in February, 1968, when the city council approved a $6000 civic center feasibility study. To keep project cost down, Sabonjian sought the cooperation of the park board. The board donated to the city the downtown park which the architects had selected as a site for the center. At this writing the mayor is using his assurances of council compliance and the availability of the property to solicit donations and long term commitments from area industries. He hopes that industries will purchase revenue bonds tied to civic center rentals and fees. Once this is done, he will proceed to acquire nearby property for parking lots, and arrange for lessees to operate facilities in the center.

Urban renewal was a case of inaction on the part of the mayor, striking in terms of the expectations of others.[3] The drive was initiated and financed by a group of downtown businessmen who became interested in federal urban renewal as a way of revitalizing downtown Waukegan. Representatives of the group visited cities which had undertaken renewal to gain preliminary information and determine what they felt were the necessary components of program success.

Initial opposition to the downtown plan ("Let the businessmen rebuild their own buildings" was a common ad) had grown more complicated with the drawing of the more inclusive Community Renewal Plan. As the controversy grew more intense, more and more issues and fears became associated with the proposal. Proponents were increasingly frustrated in their attempts to explain and sell the plan. An *unorganized* public defeated the referendum three to one.

Sabonjian explains his virtual abstention as an effort to "get out from under" an issue which he felt was a "loser."[4] The referendum was a way of avoiding identification with a highly divisive issue. Government action would have been highly visible and, as was clear from the high controversy, perceived by many as partisan. The proposal for government sponsorship of downtown renewal had immediately created a tension among groups to whom the mayor is committed. As the controversy developed, a wide array of fears and hostilities became identified with renewal. Positions were focused into zero-sum arguments and the polarities involved a large proportion of normally apolitical constituents. "Who wants to be a martyr?" asked Sabonjian remarking on the difficulties of renegotiating with these rarely involved (hard to reach) persons. "You've got to live to fight another day!"

Yet controversy is not sufficient as an index to action or inaction. Necessary innovation must at least part of the time be unpopular. Long-range objectives may incur short-run objections. What is important is, as Parsons suggested, the maintenance of balance between expenditures, accountability and gains. How many commitments and resources are involved? How predictable is the outcome of a program? How predictable is the public response? What are the costs of action in terms of alternative programs? What is the relationship in time between expenditures, return, and accountability?

Sabonjian, who says he regrets the defeat of urban renewal, suggests that, handled differently the program might have been successful.

> If they would have started on the southeast corner of the city, I would have been for it. The people would have shouted "Hosanna" when the slums disappeared and voted in the rest of the projects. As it was, they would have said, "The rich get richer and the poor get poorer."

Whether different programming would have made a difference remains unknown. The businessmen had justified putting the downtown phase of the program first on what they felt were sound economic and political grounds (the downtown plan required no local tax money and was to serve as a model for and help finance later phases of redevelopment).[5] The mayor's view was that the controversial issue was for him a political loser.

Had the mayor (rather than the downtown businessmen) planned renewal, what considerations would have been important? Ideally, the political head would prevent conflict from arising among his commitments, support what he could define as the "public good," avoid issues which divided his public, and squeeze potentially divisive issues into complementary form. These conditions of multiple gain seem to have held or been created for the incorporation of the Lakehurst shopping mall.

If a political head is unable to avoid conflict among commitments, however, *control* over that conflict becomes critical. There are several illustrative cases where Waukegan's mayor was willing to allow commitments to become problems. These cases were characterized first by relative certainty on the part of the mayor that rancor he would incur over unpopular action would be more than cancelled by subsequent support for program results, and, second, that resource involvement was not so extensive as to threaten other desired action. Controlling the scale and timing of these projects, he was confident that he could stabilize necessary relationships before political "solvency" was necessary, i.e., before election time. Resource involvement, timing, length of program realization, and certainty of results become crucial variables in the mayor's calculations.

One case where the mayor successfully "controlled" opposition was the sanitary landfill. Some new means of garbage disposal had to be implemented if the city was to avoid a serious rat problem. Some action was needed but citizens refused to approve a landfill. No ward would have it. Sabonjian, however, felt the landfill would be acceptable when completed and could be completed within his four year latitude. He rejected a proposal for a costly incinerator and went ahead (despite neighborhood outrage) with plans for a landfill in the eighth ward. The program began immediately after his election and was completed eighteen months later. Two and a half years before election, the violently opposed neighbors had come to appreciate the ball park which had been provided on the reclaimed swampland of the landfill. In the subsequent election, he won in every precinct in the city, including all of those in this neighborhood.

Within three months after his 1969 election, Sabonjian in a similar show of force approved a thirteen million dollar highrise complex in an area which had been zoned for one-family housing. Against the violent objections of ward residents (457 put their homes on the market), the mayor forged ahead with the development, convinced that objections were based on race prejudice, misinformation, and a refusal to listen to facts. In opposition to objections, Sabonjian is convinced that properties will not be devalued, that private taxes will not go up, that sewers will not be inadequate, that schools will not be overcrowded, and that apartment residents will not be irresponsible. He is convinced on the other side, that the housing shortage in Waukegan is critical and that the twenty acres of landscaping around the complex will greatly improve the appearance of a neighborhood dominated by tract housing and tiny lots. Once again, the mayor is confident he will be vindicated before the next election. In addition, he will have innovated where innovation was necessary and headed off future housing problems.

In the sense that functional innovation and constituent opinion are not nor can not be made to appear congruent, the politician has few "safe" alternatives. He has little room for experimentation with programs. If he is to act, he must be able to both predict and schedule results to conform with political necessity. If this is not possible, many politicians will take their chances with having failed to act. Urban renewal had not been formulated to prevent conflict among the mayor's commitments nor was he able to control its size or timing.

OUR FEARLESS LEADER: CONTROVERSY AND DIRECTION

The mayor's game is played most successfully in the absence of controversy. In covert dealings the mayor manipulates his stock of influence so as to make secure his position and build his action potential.

The emergence of open controversy raises the costs of action. It brings to the surface the frictions and contradictions among the politicians' various commitments and it magnifies the possibility that normally inactive constituents will become a problem. In order to minimize losses, the politician is apt to assume a stand-off position. If he is forced to impose a solution, it is usually an elaborate compromise.

The strategy is logical. If in situations of controversy, he avoids taking a position, the mayor minimizes the possibility that he will create, among either participants or constituents, antagonisms which could prove terminal to the relationship. While no participating faction may be satisfied with the mayor's neutrality, he has left the door open to future and more satisfactory dealings with each of them. While all participants may be disappointed at not receiving support in their claims, no one feels that the mayor is an *opponent*. Thus in each case the mayor can hope that there will be future opportunities to engage in negotiations which will produce more satisfactory results—thus gains in influence.

At the same time the politician has protected himself from the antagonisms he fears might develop in the constituency if he appeared to be "working for" the merchants, or the black community, or any special interest group. Again, if he is not a friend, at least he is not an enemy. By taking no stand on controversial issues, the mayor maximizes the probability that he will stay in office and he protects the relationships which make the centralization of influence possible. His strategy is aimed not at bettering his position but at holding it, not at maximizing gains but at minimizing losses.

At best, however, there will be losses. A holding strategy may reduce the most serious ones, but it creates its own. The outbreak of controversy announces that something is wrong. A holding strategy on the part of the chief executive suggests that, not only was nothing done to prevent the conflict, but nothing can be done now. For those who see the political order as efficient administration, it has failed. For those who see the political order as a conflict controlling mechanism, it has failed. For those who, like Sayre and Kaufman, feel that "the office of the Mayor is first and fundamentally a symbol of unity for the city" ("The mayor and his office are the visible expression of the city, its personification as an organized community . . .") it has failed.[6] Whether these are reasonable expectations or not, they reverberate through the community.

While Banfield argues that "according to the Chicago view . . . affected interests should work out for themselves the 'best' solution to the matter," expectations of order and direction are also pre$_\Lambda$a-lent.[7] Government may be unable to resolve issues but it is still held responsible. It is not only slum tenants and slum landlords who are blamed for slum housing, but the political order as well. It is not contractors and developers who are called upon to explain the city's growth or appearance, but the political order. When the Waukegan school board adopted sex education for the fifth and sixth grades, the mayor's office was flooded with complaints. When an odor hung over the city for several days as a result of problems at the sanitary district (a unit independent of the city), the mayor's office was the registry of complaints and demands. For the most part, it did no good to explain to irate citizens that it was not the city's fault.

Nor does Sabonjian, at least, want to pass the buck. In most cases, he prefers to convey an image that he is, indeed, the man in charge and one capable of being there. In the case of the sanitary district odor, complaining citizens were told that the mayor was doing everything possible to correct the condition. Then *he* called the sanitary district and complained.

Sabonjian often asserts his authority to the point of belligerence. When the Lake County Health Director said the Waukegan beaches should be closed due to water pollution, Sabonjian took issue. Taking full responsibility for his actions, "The mayor said he didn't agree with the tests taken and ordered . . . independent tests (7-15-69)." The county retested also and retracted; the beaches were given an all-clear. After subsequent tests, however, the county again urged closing. But:

> Mayor Robert Sabonjian of Waukegan said he has no plans to comply with the recommendation by the county health department until he has received a report from the city bacteriologist. (7-28-69)

When these tests again refuted the samplings of the Lake County Health Department, the mayor declared: "I'm getting sick and tired of hearing that Waukegan beaches are polluted—all of the sudden" (7-29-69). More tests brought the closing of the beaches —but for five days only.

After two hours of listening to explanations [from county officials] why the Lake Michigan beaches in the county might be closed up to three years, Sabonjian said he was ordering his city's beaches opened today.

"I feel satisfied our water is not polluted," the mayor said. "I feel very safe—but I will not take chances . . . tests will continue to be taken seven days a week." (8-7-69)

Citizens with flooded basements called a meeting to consider possible action concerning sewer problems. Sabonjian was not invited. In the middle of the meeting he burst in, unexpectedly, accompanied by his street superintendent and an engineer from the city's consulting firm. He took charge, telling the homeowners:

"I'm going to Washington July 25 to try to get a federal loan at low interest. I've notified our senators and representatives that I don't want just 'lip service' about money when I am in the capital."

He stated that surveys were underway and "some answers will come in about thirty days."

He noted that he was aware of the situation and that he was not at the meeting to offer any alibi. (7-16-69)

When the basements flooded he cut a trip short to be in the city when complaining citizens called. He came home from California when street violence hit the city. He climbed the fence of the football field when violence broke out at the high school homecoming game and urged calm from a microphone in the center of the field.

The mayor is present to handle small insecurities as well as large. A late evening phone call informed him that city youths were dancing in an unsafe hall. "You better close it down right now," the caller told the mayor. "The mayor immediately called a local contractor to make an 'on the spot' inspection to determine if there was any danger" (2-27-68).

A newspaper article reported another citizen's three year drive to get a road moved off of his yard. "He said he first learned of the encroachment in 1965 and since then had written letters, telephoned, and taken city officials out to lunch" (6-19-68). Finally he took the problem to the mayor.

Sabonjian said it is agreed the city has to get the road off Greisheimer's property, or buy a portion of it.

"You've been taking the wrong people to lunch," Sabonjian said. "Next time you should take me." (6-19-68)

These last two incidents are similar to the range of activities detailed in the preceding chapters. The behavior is consistently authoritative and dramatically competent.

One of Sabonjian's best gags was related to just this issue. The parade chairman at the Sesquecentennial celebration introduced the mayor who was the first speaker to address spectators from the review stand. "We must," the chairman said, "thank God for this beautiful day." Sabonjian took his position at the podium. "What do you mean?" he said, " 'Thank God for this beautiful day.' When I got up this morning and looked out the window, I said, 'Sabonjian, you've done it again.' "

The whole syndrome of personal responsibility and leadership is evident in Richard Daley's frequent statements on civil order. For example:

> I'll tell you now that as long as I am mayor of this city there will be law and order in its streets.[8]

Observers concur on the need for this stance. Robert Moses held what was probably a greater number and variety of public offices than any other individual in American history. He achieved unparalleled success in undertakings both official and unofficial.[9] This three-decade dynamo of New York City politics says of the office of the mayor:

> All efforts to shift power and responsibility to a deputy mayor or a business manager, on the false assumption that city government is just big business minus the profit motive, and to reduce the mayor to a greeter and a symbol, or to lighten his responsibilities by handing them to subordinates with a passion for anonymity—these efforts have failed because in the never-ending clinches and emergencies the people demand leadership. . . .[10]

Sayre and Kaufman observe that the mayor

> is the central focus of responsibility and accountability for all that occurs in the city: he is the problem-solver, the crisis handler, the man to blame for all the defects of the electorate, of the organized groups. . . . His office is the most perceptible, the most impressive; it is taken for granted that he has the most power and thus the capacity to act vigorously in the solution of the city's problems great and small. Failure to meet these high expectations is taken to mean not lack of vigor in the office but in the man.[11]

Dahl similarly feels that constituents hold such expectations of the mayoralty. He recounts a New Haven controversy which developed around zoning for metal houses. Throughout the controversy Mayor Celentano was indecisive. Dahl concludes:

> A few weeks later, Celentano lost the mayoralty election to Lee. The contest over the metal houses probably had little to do with the outcome, for it involved only a few hundred people. . . . It is possible, however, that the publicity about the conflict in the local press created the impression among some wavering voters that the Celentano administration suffered from a lack of drive and coordination.[12]

Sabonjian believes this kind of publicity to be serious indeed. He argues that positive press coverage is built upon control over issues. In situations the politician has not engineered, he may well be caught in a weak position. He should work, rather, to see that he is selecting the issues which will attract the attention of the press. In such cases his position is strong. He maximizes the probability that coverage of his activities will be positive.

Controversy has bad side effects on the politician's relationships with participants. The covert dealings he normally makes with these persons, particularly leaders and subleaders, cannot be carried out as they could while the public was indifferent. In the absence of controversy, the mayor worked closely with individual blacks in locating housing and fighting the housing authority. He undercut the authority of department heads and the civil service principles of "good government" in responding to the service demands of the middle class. He worked closely with business and industry to improve downtown parking, install new lighting, finance the Centennial, bring new industries to Waukegan, acquire a marina, and retain the courthouse. He approved the landscaping for public use of property although the property could be reclaimed by the original owner. All of these actions served the purposes of the mayor. Had controversy focused attention on them, they might well have become impossible. In the last case, for example, positive results were two. The industrialist found himself delighted with his new front yard; the public with the new look at the lakefront. Were the project made overt, however, one might expect considerable opposition. One would not be surprised at least if the average citizen objected to the use of tax money for such purposes.

Yet numerous decisions about such matters as zoning ordinances, sewerage extensions and road construction are made daily in accordance with the wishes of those who have established channels for reaching political goals. The net gain for the politician in rewarding subleaders, placating pressure groups, or ingratiating wealth and power with such inconspicuous favors as those mentioned above can only be positive. Indeed these are frequently neat ways of "authorizing" others to pay for civic improvements.

Controversy inhibits this behavior. Relationships with participants are sacrificed. While the mayor may assume that he will have future opportunities to stabilize the commitments he must sacrifice during controversy, his position for the time at least is not good. Finally, controversy has inhibiting effects on desired programs. The mayor said he would have liked to see urban renewal pass had there been less dissent. Had similar controversy developed around the shopping mall, it is unlikely that the mayor could have pushed through the necessary council ordinances without charges of a rubber stamp council and a dictatorial mayor.

From the standpoint of executive preference, highly controversial issues are political mistakes. The politician's best strategy, given special interest disputes, may be to espouse the lowest common denominator of perceived public opinion (usually the *status quo*) over the desires of particularistic groups. *Prevention* of controversy is usually better. Assuming that special groups are going to propose special interests which will be opposed by other special interests, there are still alternatives available to a mayor who would like to control the eruption of controversy. There are techniques which he uses to control the outbreak of controversy so that he can retain the issue-focusing function for himself.

THE MAYOR'S GAME:
MANAGING CONFLICT AND DEFINING ISSUES

The politician can prevent controversy if he can anticipate points of friction and minimize them by finding a common ground where action is not a flat acceptance or rejection of one or another position. If he can define the issue in such a way that the goals of various groups do not appear to be strictly inconsistent, he can head off controversy. If the issue is not settled in its early stages and factions turn for support to the general populace, controversy may cause the politician to fear any action and to lose all control over outcome.

This view is diametrically opposed to that of Banfield who argues that:

> The political head is . . . inclined to let a civic controversy develop in its own way without interference from him, in the expectation that 'public opinion' (the opinion of 'civic leaders' and the newspapers) will 'crystalize.' Controversies . . . serve the function of forming and preparing opinion; they are the process by which an initial diversity of views and interests is reduced to the point where a political head feels that the 'community' is 'behind' the project.[13] [In this model, civic associations and newspapers are assumed to collectively embody or represent the 'public interest.'][14]
>
> When agreement is reached, or when the process of controversy has gone as far as it can, he ratifies the agreement and carries it into effect.[15]

In Waukegan there is evidence of behavior inconsistent with Banfield's generalization.

During the summer of 1968, the U.S. Department of Defense issued an order designed to minimize racial discrimination in military housing. It required landlords who rent to military families to sign statements pledging non-discriminatory rental policies. It prohibited Navy families from renting apartments from landlords who would not sign such pledges. The ruling had clear applicability in Waukegan where many of the families stationed at Great Lakes Naval Training Center rent apartments. The issue carried a high controversy potential. Conflict was apt to develop between landlords and military officials—perhaps resulting in the relocation of many Navy families. Conflict could develop in the buildings and neighborhoods where there were Navy rentals. The issue might stir up interest in and opposition to the more general issue of open-housing in the community. All of these positions would be likely to elicit support from sympathetic factions throughout the city.

It would be difficult for the mayor to take a stand on such an issue. For all practical purposes he was never required to do so since the issue was eliminated before it had a chance to become controversial. The mayor called a quiet meeting of all landlords. He explained that the Navy had announced an open-housing policy which required them to sign contracts in which they pledged to rent on a non-discriminatory basis. The mayor realized that there would be opposition from some of them. It would, however, be highly unfortunate, for both the city and the landlords, if trouble should develop around Navy housing. In point of fact, he wanted them to understand there was really very little threat involved. There were only half a dozen black Navy families renting in the entire area. Surely the problem could be worked out. The mayor, certainly, had no intention of making an issue of such contracts. He was sure that the black families could be housed without any hostile landlord being forced to rent. Thus, the landlords (some very hostile to the idea) signed the agreement. No conflict developed. Navy housing was safeguarded. A potentially controversial ruling had crept into the Waukegan housing code. Sabonjian had disappointed no one. There was no issue. The blacks were housed.

On another occasion, representatives of a black citizens' group appeared with demands that Sabonjian appoint several black members to the school board. Sabonjian stated that he intended to appoint one, that one black board member would be proportionate to the black population percentage, and that any more would provoke rumblings in other ethnic groups and in the white community. He had to appoint members representing the range of population groups, surely they could understand his problem. The mayor added, however, that he would like to use this opportunity to discuss ways in which the city and the black community might work together in ways which would not elicit destructive opposition. They knew as well as he that white forces would object to the city's responding to petitions and demands (as for school board appointees). Such opposition could make all action impossible. If, on the other hand, these men would work with instead of against the mayor (thus allowing him to avoid destructive opposition), gains could be made. If, for example, they could arrange for volunteer counselors to staff a summer camp, he could arrange for lakeside property to be set aside for the camp. He could get industries to donate boats, playground equipment and other necessary supplies. Or if they preferred they could work together on renovating South side homes. Such projects would not cause conflict. If, on the other hand, they insist on radical change, they might well put the mayor in a position where he could not act at all.

Dahl states quite explicitly that Mayor Lee used similar strategies when confronted with special interest proposals which he expected would elicit opposition if allowed to develop. Because of their narrow popularity, such proposals are not the type of issue Lee cared to deploy his resources to realize. Yet he would prefer not to let the controversy develop uncontrolled either. Dahl says of Lee:

> possibly as much by temperament as by his experience of an electoral defeat that could be regarded as sheer chance, he was prone to worry about the dangers of unexpected and uncontrolled events. . . . His political skills included a . . . labor mediator's ability to head off controversy by mutual understanding, compromise, negotiating and bargaining.[16]

Dahl speaks, also, about Lee's "unremitting search for measures that will unify rather than disrupt the alliance," and his "unusual skill at negotiating agreement and damping down potential disagreements before they flared into opposition. . . ."[17]

Another story about Mayor Lee puts this in rather amusing context. Allan R. Talbot talks about the strangeness of the Lee coalition.

> "Group dynamics" is what he [Mayor Lee] would call it, but whatever it was, the careful courting of the voters, the personal link with Yale, the creation of a pro-administration business organization, the accommodation with the politicians, and control of the bureaucracy had the practical effect of immobilizing his opposition, giving him the support he needed, and creating apparent consensus. From afar the Lee coalition seemed to have the order, body, and unity of a symphony. But in many ways it was a one-man act with Lee assuming the combined role of composer, arranger, conductor, and performer.[18]

The importance to all this of Lee's defining the situation became quite obvious, Talbot goes on, at the annual birthday party which Lee supporters held in honor of the mayor.

> The parties were usually held in the fading ballroom of the Hotel Taft and attended by about three hundred key persons. Up the small cramped hotel elevators they would silently ascend, eyeball to neck, then alight and move into the ballroom to find the table where their group was sitting. There was never enough room, so the overflows created unlikely table partners. One could find a fire marshal

next to a law professor, a bank president seated next to a ward heeler, a League of Women Voters member next to Arthur Barbeiri, or a *Register* reporter next to a young Redevelopment Agency staff man. The three man string ensemble would play "Marching Along Together" which was suffered in grim silence. . . There in the Taft ballroom the coalition was out of place and function. Its members belonged in their natural community setting linked only by Lee, and their purpose was not to bestow gifts on the leader but to play the mayor's game.[19]

T. Harry Williams in his biography of Huey Long suggests that Long's Louisiana organization required the same sort of control over definitions.

Huey deliberately kept his top group formless. . . . He knew that he could not bring his men together in a close arrangement. . . They were, in truth, a strange assortment of political bedfellows, men of varied backgrounds and beliefs, striking refutations of the theory that political groups are held together by a common ideology. They included radical neo-Populists from the country parishes, equally radical Share Our Wealthers, stanch conservatives with links to business from New Orleans or other cities, professional politicians who were interested primarily in spoils, and professional idealists who gained in Longism a vision of a utopian Louisiana. Huey had to keep these people "on different levels." Another man when his attention was called to this problem of Huey's said "Yes, and the wonderful thing was that he had us in our places but never let us get together so that we could fight each other and mess up his show."[20]

A politician whose cage of pressures and whose effective resources are constituted by diverse and potentially conflicting groups can not afford to "let controversy develop in its own way." Perhaps also new meaning could be attached to Machiavelli's "divide and conquer."

Note on Violence When the processes of political controversy break down, violence may occur as an alternative means of expressing or resolving differences and perhaps of achieving goals. It is this form of dissension that is most specifically the responsibility of the executive. This is true in fact and in expectation. Violence is not simply competition among groups, but rejection of government prescription. Groups are necessarily in opposition to rule by law as it is promulgated and administered in the community.

Moreover, civil order is, by and large, considered by constituents to be the first and minimum responsibility of government. Its absence indicates not only lack of direction from government and lack of community integration, but also government's inability to function at a minimum level of effectiveness. Most constituents will find this unpalatable and most will hold the executive accountable. Since the range of constituents who will be dissatisfied is so inclusive, violence is avoided if at all possible—sometimes at great cost.

As an official responsibility of government, the maintenance of order has constitutionally provided instrumentalities. One of these, of course, is the police. Adequate and visible policemen are frequently thought to be important in the avoidance of violence. In his statement calling up the National Guard for service at the 1968 Democratic Convention, Daley expressed this view.

> I think some people who might cause trouble won't do it if the proper precautions have been taken.

> This administration has always taken the position that an ounce of protection is worth a pound of cure.[21]

Sabonjian takes much this same position. He many times stated that the city would not tolerate disorder; when worried he took the steps to back up this warning (supplying and riot training his own police, alerting the National Guard) and he made known among relevant audiences the steps he had taken.

Positive prevention techniques may resemble those used to cool out controversy—compromise proposals. But Sabonjian's notion of positive prevention includes also his drive to supply job opportunities and recreational facilities. He runs an office employment agency, recruits industries to Waukegan, sponsors training programs and fights for fair employment opportunities. Sabonjian is constantly seeking ways of expanding recreational facilities. He introduced a city-sponsored lake front dance pavillion for teens; he sees the civic center as a recreational nirvana; he frequently proposes to persons he thinks might be interested that they consider running (with his assistance) a dance hall or teen club.

Whether negative or positive, prevention techniques require accurate information both in and out of the mayor's office. If unrest is known, or subversive organization is identified, action can be taken: force can be displayed, pressure can be applied, alternatives can be offered, agreements can be reached. Sabonjian has finely developed techniques for collecting and sending out information. He describes his relationship with the south side:

> They've got a power structure down there too—it's not the people you'd think, but I grew up down there and know a lot of people. When things get shaky, these are the people who know what's going to happen. I've ears down there. When I hear there may be trouble, I call up these leaders and ask them if there's anything to it and if there is, I ask them to go over and straighten it out.

The message here includes pre-emptive compromises, reminders of the advantages to be had with cooperation and the losses involved in opposition.

If early information is disturbing or inadequate, Sabonjian will call in F.B.I. investigators. On at least two occasions, this was the case. The result of one investigation was greater preparedness and the result of the other a cooling out of fears.

The street disorders which in 1966 brought Waukegan wide news coverage began during Sabonjian's California vacation. He has subsequently taken steps to cover himself for this contingency; his trips are shorter now and unpublicized. When violence does occur, Sabonjian has two alternatives open to him. He can use police force to terminate or at least curtail violence. Last minute compromises may similarly come into play. Week-long disturbances in Waukegan's high school over the selection of the 1967 homecoming court were followed by an announcement that an agreement which had been worked out by the mayor and a black leader would assure a peaceful homecoming.

Sabonjian is opposed to what he considers to be over-eager reporting of civil disturbances including vandalism. When the city gardener suggested that the mayor request the newspaper to print a picture of a bed of newly planted flowers which had been chopped down by vandals, Sabonjian said no. "That would start it up all over town. Just put in more flowers." After the mayor had convinced himself that SDS organizers were not a threat to his administration or the integration of the community (and could not be treated as such), he urged strongly that they be ignored lest city action feed their cause.

Summary Controversy has many costly effects for the political head. It inhibits covert agreements and thus the success of action programs. It is destructive of actual and symbolic community unity. It takes direction out of the mayor's hands and places it elsewhere. The mayor not only appears as an ineffectual player but in fact loses his chances for effective action. It is to the advantage of the mayor to foresee and head off controversy with early compromises. If he is to do this he must have an information network which will give him early knowledge of emerging dissent and he must have the wherewithal to offer attractive alternatives to replace the original goals of conflicting groups.

Violence is a still more damaging possibility. It shares the negative implications of controversy and also includes a performance breakdown at the very core of constituent expectations—basic civil order. It involves more than conflict among groups; it involves violation of government prescription. Violence as a form of dissent cannot be ignored but must be handled by the executive. The less attention disorder and confusion elicit, however, the more effective the administration appears. Dissipation of dissent through early settlement based on early and accurate information is invaluable. In addition, mechanisms of control (official and unofficial) become more appropriate.

THE MAYOR'S PROGRAM: SPONSORING PROJECTS AND FOCUSING ATTENTION

The politician wants to avoid controversy but he wants also to act and to lead. This means not only a protective desire to avoid charges of ineffectuality but also a positive desire to appear effectual. Lasswell and Kaplan note that apathy, like open hatred, undermines the stability of an administration, for officialdom "requires continued support against the potential threat of rival elites."[22] Thus the mayor needs attention-getting programs which will arouse support and enthusiasm for his administration. For community attention, the political head will seek programs with potentially wide support. Further, he will seek to retain the issue defining and issue focusing role for himself in order that his multiple reward definitions remain dominant.

Hopefully the executive will have reassuring information indicating that a proposal will be well received. There are two ways in which the mayor can locate such areas. One is that described by Banfield; the other described by Dahl. In the Banfield model, the executive is passive but in some cases does end up with agreed upon programs he can then adopt and claim. In the Dahl model, the mayor formulates programs he believes will be widely agreeable.

Banfield asserts that Mayor Daley waits for formal organizations and civic associations to devise, propose, adapt and agree upon programs he can then rubber stamp and be assured of political payoff.

> Wanting to do big things and not caring very much which ones, the political head will be open to suggestions. . . . He will be receptive, particularly, to proposals from people who are in a position to guarantee that successful action will win a "seal of approval" from some of the "good government" groups [Banfield feels civic programs are directed to getting the support of these groups. In this model the machine controls the inner city wards who need not be considered much in program selection]. . . . A plan made by the big business organizations, the civic associations and the newspapers is sure to be acclaimed. From the political head's standpoint it is sure-fire, for the people who make it and the people who will pass judgment upon it are the same.[23]

Indeed this is one way to discover areas of agreement. The compromise proposal of a resolved controversy is likely to be one with political payoff.

Dahl emphasizes a quite different style of program adoption, but describes a model, the "petty sovereignties" pattern, which is similar to Banfield's. "Petty sovereignties" is Dahl's term for uncoordinated power centers (e.g. mayor, city agencies) which have generally accepted but not formally distinct spheres of influence. When conflict occurs among groups seeking approval from such centers, resolution occurs by the groups' simply "fighting it out" for there is no power capable of coordinating the independent power centers.[24] While Dahl describes the petty sovereignties pattern of decision-making as existing in the absence of enterprising leadership (in this case historically prior to Mayor Lee's administration), it is also issue-specific. Sabonjian clearly let petty sovereignties "fight it out" on several occasions. Banfield's data on Chicago decisions are similarly illustrative. Even the most powerful political figures will select carefully the instances in which they will undertake centralized direction. The petty sovereignties pattern, then, is a weak or tardy way of locating agreement. It is used when there is no power capable of more aggressive action or when leaders possessing such capability choose not to employ it because in their estimation the odds of community consensus seem low. In such cases executive adoption of programs occurs when and if special interests can demonstrate internal agreement and external support.

The alternative Dahl proposes to this model of after-the-fact adoption is one in which the politician is himself the primary initiator and the pivotal figure in the adoption of proposals and the realization of community programs.

> Neither in 1950 nor in later years was there anything like a discernible popular demand for measures to reverse the physical and economic decay of New Haven, though citizens were evidently discontented with the city in various ways. . .
>
> It is impossible to say with confidence how important these worries over New Haven were to its citizens, but it is reasonable to suppose that for most people they were at a low level of urgency. Thus the feeling that something had to be done about New Haven was latent; it was potential rather than existing; agreement on a strategic plan had to be created. *It would be wrong to suppose, then, that politicians were pressed into action by public demand. On the contrary, they had to sniff the faint smell of distant political success, generate the demands, and activate the latent consensus.*[25]

It was Mayor Lee himself who set about to sniff out discontent, generate demands, activate consensus and create agreement on a strategic plan. He succeeded because:

> He possessed a detailed knowledge of the city and its people, a formidable information-gathering system, and an unceasing, fulltime preoccupation with all the aspects of his job.[26]

More specific tactics for locating areas of unrest or desire can be identified: Sabonjian's open-door office policy and his strategic network of reliable informants, like Lee's use of the sample survey, bring in information which can be used in discovering the grounds for acceptable proposals.

In addition, boards and commissions, carefully selected for representativeness, both front for administration policies and provide a testing ground for aspects of the program as they evolve. Says Dahl of Lee's Citizens' Action Commission for Redevelopment:

. . . properly used, the CAC was a mechanism not for *settling* disputes but for *avoiding* them altogether. The Mayor and the Development Administrator believed that whatever received the assent of the CAC would not be strongly opposed by other elements in the community. Their estimate proved to be correct. And the reason was probably not so much the direct influence over public opinion of the CAC collectively or its members individually, as it was that the CAC *was* public opinion; that is, its members represented and reflected the main sources of articulate opinion in the political stratum of New Haven. The Mayor and the Development Administrator used the CAC to test the acceptability of their proposals to the political stratum; in fact, the very existence of the CAC and the seemingly ritualistic process of justifying all proposals to its members meant that members of the administration shaped their proposals according to what they expected would receive the full support of the CAC and therefore of the political stratum. The Mayor, who once described himself as an 'expert in group dynamics,' was particularly skillful in estimating what the CAC could be expected to support or reject. If none of the administration's proposals on redevelopment and renewal were ever opposed by the CAC, the explanation probably lies less in the Mayor's skill in the art of persuasion than in his capacity for judging with considerable precision what the existing beliefs and commitments of the men on the CAC would compel them to agree to if a proposal were presented in the proper way, time, and place.[27]

Sabonjian uses also direct if informal means of testing ideas on constituents. "You sense the pulse," he says. "You pay attention to the guy on the street—how he reacts to you, what he says when you ask him if he's for you or if he likes what you're doing. You make yourself available and you listen to the people. I knew I wouldn't have trouble running Republican, for example, because of the way people I asked reacted."[28]

The mayor drops proposals which this trial and error method tell him do not have a future. At one point, for example, he urged local radio listeners to circulate petitions demanding state judicial reform. Those who were interested were to contact his office. Two persons called in. Sabonjian presumably got the same reaction from persons on the street. The mayor's drive for the blue ballot was not mentioned again.

On another occasion, he proposed that something had to be done for young people. He took up the battle to open a "drag strip" for teens.

> A $200,000 drag strip was proposed for the old Waukegan Airport.
> . . . Sabonjian said this is a tremendously popular form of enter-
> tainment particularly for the younger set. . . .
>
> "I get sick and tired of hearing people always pointing out the
> faults of our teen-agers. I think it's high time if we're so doggoned
> smart and know everything the kids are doing wrong that we should
> have something better to offer.
>
> "I think we should stop criticizing and start pooling our talents."
> He said the drag strip would pay for itself. (4-67)

The proposal didn't seem to bring out many proponents and neighborhood residents were furious.

> A proposed drag strip on Waukegan's northwest side came to a
> skidding halt Wednesday night after hitting a solid wall of opposi-
> tion. . . .
>
> "If I thought for one minute I was going to cause so much con-
> cern to so many property owners I would not have made statements
> that might have sounded so definite," Sabonjian told the group.
> (7-6-67)

If the politician's original guess about citizen desire is incorrect,
this preliminary testing allows him time to get out gracefully—
before boards are appointed and potential opposition has something firm to oppose. He can catch mistakes here, affirm his willingness to listen to opposition, and get out before real controversy
has the materials it needs to develop.

The projects which have held Sabonjian's attention have been:
economic growth and prosperity, city beautification, housing for
the elderly, the civic center, shopping malls, road improvements,
improved snow removal service, law and order, and a sanitary
landfill which turned a city dump into a baseball park. The
mayor's campaign letters in 1969 summarized: "I have tried hard
to be a good mayor and have worked toward making Waukegan
a safe and beautiful place in which to live." No other claims
were made.

The programs which have made Waukegan's mayor so intensely
popular may in other cities be associated with other government
officials. Sayre and Kaufman attribute the remarkable success of
the Robert Moses tenure in New York City to its association with
popular and visible programs.

> The reputations enjoyed by members of the Port Authority and by
> Commissioner Robert Moses rest in considerable part upon the fact

that people use, see, enjoy, and benefit from the facilities to which their names are attached. The tunnels and bridges, highways and parks and playgrounds and beaches testify to millions of citizens that these are men who get things done.[29]

Another form of visibility is publicity. On the one hand this implies the executive's presentation of programs. On the other, it means coverage of those programs in the mass media.

With regard to program presentation, the tactics of Robert Moses are again instructive.

> The first thing Moses does when the time is right to start something is to get it clearly in focus for everyone likely to be concerned. This means that while he has been doing his own casting about he has had studies made—often elaborate and costly ones—as to the feasibility of the project, its best structure and method, and its permanent value. When he goes to his bankers and begins to ask for authority from the appropriate bodies, he is ready with the kind of publicity which it seems churlish to oppose.
>
> The Moses pamphlet is really formidable. . . . It can be understood at a sharp glance. Pictorial charts and superb photographs are accompanied by descriptive sentences that are little more than captions. Predictions are unequivocal.
>
> The impact of this reporting is tremendous. It creates confidence, it builds pride. As a result, when another project is proposed, the original doubts are bound to be less than they would otherwise have been. In New York, anything Moses wants to do is presumed to be worth doing. The faint voices of objectors are carried away on the wind of his propaganda.[30]

These techniques are characteristics of Sabonjian salesmanship once he has decided to realize a project. He frames proposals in terms of their community value and conscientiously opposes any involvement which might smack of private gain or special interest. Sabonjian, like Moses, had an easy-to-understand pamphlet which described the civic center plan distributed far in advance of solicitations. At a meeting with the council finance committee, the civic center architect and various subleaders, Sabonjian argued with emphatic closure against the groups raising any reservations whatsoever about the proposed civic center. The way to see a program through, he insisted, was to begin the sales program as if the goal were nearly accomplished. He urged them not to raise objections or point out complications which, while themselves soluble, might raise fears among sponsors and constituents which could constitute insurmountable opposition. With a positive approach, he urged, the persons whose contributions were needed for the center's realization would stampede the city's officials in an effort to get on the bandwagon. If on the other hand, they feared the center might be a losing proposition, no one would make the early contributions and enthusiastic endorsements needed to launch an early momentum. If success appeared to be assured, industrialists would be eager to buy the bonds which would finance the center. If, in turn, industry financing was assured, taxpayer groups would have no reason to organize opposition to anticipated taxpayer costs.

Banfield documents a case where just such indecision was decisive in a project's failing. The proposal for the Fort Dearborn project in Chicago failed as much as anything else because no one was willing to make the first commitment, to take the step which would demonstrate confidence in the success of the enterprise.[31]

In addition to the method in which the executive presents his programs, the coverage newsmen give them is critical to positive reception. In this regard, we have already discussed the importance of the politician himself selecting the issues which will attract the attention of the press. When one has engineered the situation, he deals from his greatest strength. For Sabonjian this means that one's programs and one's person so dominate the scene that other information sources are, in effect, choked. Sabonjian commented on his tactics with regard to the formerly hostile but now quite tractable Waukegan press:

> You've got to capture the imagination of the press. You decide what goes into the paper because what you're doing is too good not to report. Take LaGuardia—reading the comics and following fire engines—It was great stuff for the New York press—the greatest stuff they'd seen. First you make sure that the people are going to respond in ways you want the press to report. (And you do that by keeping in touch with them. Nobody jeers or heckles when I talk somewhere.) Then you give them something to report.

The newspaper reporter who covered City Hall in Waukegan seconded Sabonjian's view.

> With a subject like Sabonjian to cover, you never run out of good newspaper copy. It's all you can do just to keep up with him. Most reporters have to really look for stories—or create them. The

————— is known for this. Its reporters use the paper's position as a communications center to seek out points of possible friction and stir up the trouble. Then they report it. You never need to stir up action if you're covering Sabonjian.

The reporter commented further on Sabonjian's openness as a reason for his good relations with the press. He gives newsmen sufficient facts to satisfy them that they are getting their story.

Politicians have used various means of focusing attention on themselves and their programs. The sheer enormity of Mayor Lee's efforts to remodel New Haven and his central position in the program suggest one way of spotlighting. Other, more personalized techniques are also possible and frequently less dangerous. Banfield notes that: "Moses . . . had the sharpest tongue in New York, something which assured him attention in the press."[32] Moses, in turn, commented in this way on LaGuardia's attention-catchers:

Much has been made of LaGuardia's amusing antics, whether calculated or the result of surplus energy—rushing to fires, reading the comics, leading the band, helping Grover Whalen to greet trained seals fresh from swimming the English Channel, jeering at stuffy tycoons knee deep in soft rugs in Park and Fifth Avenue Clubs, or at 'tinhorns' in the less elegant bistros, . . . acting as committing magistrate to pillory a welfare inspector who did a favor for somebody on relief, brewing beer at 115th Street and Lenox Avenue to the delight of Harlem, . . . driving the gay hurdy-gurdies from the street, screaming obscenities at Mussolini's Virginio Gayda over the Italian transatlantic radio, . . . taking away policemen's clubs, directing traffic. . . .[33]

V. O. Key reports in the same terms on Mr. Crump, the boss who for several decades dominated politics in Tennessee:

Annually he stages a boat ride for orphans and shut-ins. Free candy, apples, cookies, and soda pop are featured. When the circus comes to town Mr. Crump takes with him the same boys and girls. "And I'll have more fun than all the rest of them together," he said in 1946 as he reserved 361 seats. Let a home burn and Crump will send checks to the unfortunate. An indubitably generous spirit of beneficence redounds to organization advantage.[34]

V. O. Key notes further what may be an important determinant of the LaGuardian model of flamboyant politics or the Lee model of political leadership (in addition to the special form of courage required by each). Commenting on the personalized styles common in Alabama politics, he suggests that "perhaps a clue to the picturesque quality of many southern political leaders lies in the fact that attention attracting antics function as a substitute for party machinery in the organization of support."[35]

Lee's party was weak; LaGuardia's stand was frequently hostile to the regular party organizations; Crump's machine was a personal organization; Sabonijan is a non-party leader. Control over press releases is no doubt useful to all political executives. Yet, politicians like Mayor Daley who head firm and enduring party machinery may find themselves less vulnerable to and therefore less interested in their media image. It is easy to believe that priorities could vary widely.

Sabonjian, whether or not it is related to his non-party position, uses both issues and antics as means of focusing attention. In addition to his own projects, he is frequently identified with those of others. When the park district proposed its master plan, Sabonjian offered to assist park development by turning city property over to the park district. "I would have no hesitation in turning city property over to the park district," Sabonjian said, "if it would help them get funds any faster."

The headline read: SABONJIAN BACKS PROPOSED MASTER PLAN FOR PARKS (3-17-67) When the Lake County Community Action Project proposed a teen job center, Sabonjian offered to find office space and again stole the show: MAYOR BACKS IDEA OF TEEN JOB CENTER: ASKS FOR AID (6-67) The mayor's flamboyance usually accounts for the shift in attention toward himself. "Give'em a show," he says often—and he does just that. He rampages about voter apathy, lack of public spirit, communist influence, rioters, and bad court decisions. He came into office with a campaign against vice and syndicated crime. He on one occasion joined the police in a late night chase.

When volunteers from the Lake County Contractors Association and the Painters and Decorators Union painted the halfway house, the newspaper picture showed Sabonjian painting too. "Mayor Sabonjian," the caption explained, "is second from the top on the second ladder from right." (7-17-68) At the beginning of Cleanup Week in Waukegan, a large newspaper picture showed the director of public works coming down the street with brooms.

Sabonjian accompanied him pushing a wheelbarrow with an alderman in it. (6-17-68) When the mayor made it possible for a girl's drill team to come into Waukegan by suggesting a teen hop to raise funds, the picture which announced the group's arrival showed Sabonjian and a drill team member high stepping on the city hall yard. (4-16-69)

Sabonjian makes the newspaper when, after running into a group of students at a restaurant, he takes them back to his office for a tour or when he discovers a bad barber chair at a boys' school and gets a new one donated. He makes the news eating steak at the junior class fish fry, releasing election balloons in city neighborhoods, and collecting the "Armenian of the Year" award. When former Waukeganites arranged to host at their downstate motel ambulatory patients from Great Lakes Naval Hospital, Sabonjian arranged for box lunches to go with the sailors on the bus and he loaded himself, his wife and his children onto the bus to accompany the group. When a sanitary land fill was completed and equipped for little league baseball, Sabonjian threw a party— serving tea and crumpets on the clean site residents had said would remain a dump under Sabonjian's plan. Besides refreshments, the mayor's party featured a brass band and exhibition baseball. When a Chicago disc jockey used "There is no Waukegan" as a standard gag line on his show, Sabonjian came to the support of local teen listeners. This letter went to the disc jockey:

Dear Ron:

There are several irate and concerned teenagers in our community who take exception to your references that, "There is no Waukegan."

While I agree in your right to have a little fun, I must go alongside of those concerned. Those who are outstanding living proof that there is a Waukegan, to mention just a few, are: Otto Graham, great all time pro; Jack Benny; Pat Nugent; and, oh yes, even Mr. Mathon, who you Chicagoans must depend upon for your weather forecasts.

Have Fun! With kindest regards, I remain,

Robert Sabonjian
Mayor of the City of Waukegan
(108 years old; the city that is)

Occasionally press centrality produces unintended events. In a newspaper column called "The Hot Line" a local commentator rounds up civic gossip, applauds civic spirit and presses for moral reform. On August 9, 1968, the following story appeared in this column.

DECISIVE SABONJIAN TAKES FAST ACTION

I received a phone call Tuesday from a woman complaining about a photograph displayed in front of the Times theater, Waukegan. . .

At City Hall I picked up Mayor Sabonjian so he could pass judgment on the question of whether or not such a picture should be on display on the city's main business street.

When he saw the photo the mayor's reaction was swift. His first thought was to close the theater that very day. He was advised by an attorney that such action probably couldn't be taken under our present interpretation of what is and isn't obscene.

Sabonjian wasted no time getting rid of the picture, though. He couldn't get a key to open the large display frame holding the picture so he pried it open and removed the objectionable photo.

Many persons failed to identify with or be amused by this bit of flamboyance. The action provoked wide controversy. Letters flooded the newspaper. In them the mayor was charged with vandalism, arrogance, suppression of freedom and taking the law into his own hands. One vitriolic letter came from an alderman. A member of the Civil Board of Decency resigned, citing as reasons: 1) The mayor's appointed chairman had not convened a board meeting in two years 2) Matters such as that described in "The Hot Line" should be referred to the Board and not handled personally by the mayor.

The mayor had "given them a show" all right but a much bigger show than he intended and with unintended effects. Although a great many citizens rose in his defense—writing supportive letters to the editor and calling or writing the office—his actions had produced useless if not damaging controversy. The mayor preferred now for the storm to die out. To encourage a quick death he avoided all comment. The newspaper editor answered a letter of protest with a one line note which stated that Sabonjian had permission from the building's owner to remove the poster. Nevertheless, a group of aldermen wrote a resolution which by council vote would censure the alderman who had attacked the mayor in the newspaper letter. They delivered a copy to the Mayor with the suggestion that they would like to bring it up at that evening's meeting. The mayor said he would prefer not. Council members were urged to drop the issue.

This did not, however, prevent the Lake County Coroner from demanding the council floor and issuing a passionate defense of Mayor Sabonjian. With tears rolling down his face, the coroner charged the alderman with undermining the morals of the country, with "being against Christ, Motherhood and the American way of life" (8-24-68). Those who had fought and died in American wars, he said, to protect American values could not condone indecency. The usually vociferous mayor was conspicuously silent —some thought embarrassed. With a final editorial and a newspaper cartoon, the issue at last ended.

Sayre and Kaufman conceive control over the press as a potential of what they call the "chief-of-state" (chief of ceremony) function of the mayoralty. By and large, they feel, it is a missed potential.

> No mayor (except La Guardia on occasion) has conceived the opportunities of the chief-of-state function as Theodore Roosevelt and Woodrow Wilson grasped those of the press and the presidency, or as Al Smith used the pubic forum during his governorship, Franklin D. Roosevelt, the press and radio, and television. . . .
>
> Being poorly conceived of by the Mayors, the chief-of-state function has quite naturally been poorly staffed and poorly managed. Thus, the Mayor's press conferences . . . have evolved in forms more convenient to the press than to serve the purposes of the Mayor. They are frequent, unscheduled, unplanned, episodic, the initiative as to time and content belonging more often to the press corps than to the Mayor. The morning's news stories and editorials more often set the day's agenda for the Mayor and his staff.[36]

Control over coverage in the media allows a politician to draw the public's attention to those aspects of community life and political activity which he wishes to spotlight; it allows him to divert attention from those aspects he prefers to suppress. This is true of his own programs and images. It is also true of his boosterism for the community contributions of others. The mayor's presence increases the probability that the groups he chooses to sponsor will get good press coverage. A mayor is a useful friend of civic organizations if the press goes where he goes. This usefulness in turn provides him with a lever in the determination of civic programs.

There are enormous personal payoffs in this style of politics. The mayor is personalizing his job and his community. And he is entertaining himself and others (e.g. volunteer painters) as well as the press.

SUMMARY

The mayor hopes to select and carry out programs which will be widely popular. He uses the consensus of voluntary organizations as one way of locating areas of agreement; he uses informants, surveys, and personal availability as others. He tests proposals he believes fill his needs on boards and commissions he feels represent public opinion and he tests them on constituents directly. Among acceptable proposals, he seeks out those which will be most visible and most popular. Frequently the results of mayoral programs are physical. Publicity is another way they become noticeable through both the executive's presentation and the media's reporting. The mayor's presentation is designed to sell his programs on merits "which it seems churlish to oppose." Actual reporting is dependent upon good relations with the press. These are created and maintained over time. The politicians discussed here keep reporters so busy and columns so lively as to make the creating of issues impractical and attention to opposition unproductive.

NOTES

[1] Peter Blau, *Exchange and Power in Social Life*, (John Wiley, 1967), pp. 135–6.

[2] Talcott Parsons, "On the Concept of Influence," *Public Opinion Quarterly* (1963): 59–60.

[3] For reference to research into urban renewal see footnote 4 *supra*, Introduction.

[4] The mayor gave renewal a nominal endorsement but employed none of his well known campaign techniques to see it passed. In 1967, for example, the mayor's off-year election tactics included the following: Before the primary and final elections, he sent letters to every home in the particular ward asking the residents to vote for the candidate he preferred. Letters asked voters to vote for the candidates with whom the mayor could work; he had already, of course, had a great deal to say about the success achieved by the incumbent in performing to the satisfaction of his constituents. The mayor further contacted various group and organization leaders with requests that they assist him

in achieving the desired electoral results. The Puerto Rican and Mexican leaders, knocked on the door of every Puerto Rican and Mexican home in the city. For other issues, it should be remembered, the mayor can turn to the aldermen themselves to bring out the right vote.

[5] Waukegan already had a $300,000 public investment in the downtown area which would satisfy the federal government's demand that one-third of the loss incurred by urban renewal be paid by the local community. Thus if the downtown area project was begun before the credit expired, no additional local funds would be needed. Moreover, with a minimum displacement of persons and developers and tenants all lined up for this project (work had begun on this project in 1961 when it was still conceived as a neighborhood renewal plan) supporters hoped it could be accomplished with ease which would inspire faith in the workability of urban renewal generally. Finally it was reasoned that the increase in the highly assessed downtown tax base would make the financing of the remaining projects possible at a minimal cost to the community residents.

[6] Wallace S. Sayre and Herbert Kaufman, *Governing New York City* (Russell Sage, 1960), p. 657.

[7] Banfield, *Political Influence*, pp. 270–1.

[8] *Chicago Tribune*, 7-1-65; *Chicago Daily News*, 7-27-67; *New York Times*, 8-27-68; *Chicago Tribune*, 7-28-68.

[9] See Rexford Tugwell, "The Moses Effect," in *Urban Government*, ed. Edward Banfield (Free Press, 1961), p. 463.

[10] Robert Moses, *LaGuardia: A Salute and a Memoir* (Simon & Schuster, 1957), p. 24.

[11] Sayre and Kaufman, p. 657.

[12] Dahl, *Who Governs*, p. 197.

[13] Banfield, *Political Influence*, p. 253.

[14] *Ibid.*, p. 339.

[15] *Ibid.*, p. 253.

[16] Dahl, *Who Governs*, p. 119.

[17] *Ibid.*, pp. 202, 310.

[18] Allan R. Talbot, *The Mayor's Game* (Harper-Row, 1967), p. 99.

[19] *Ibid.*, p. 100.

[20] T. Harry Williams, *Huey Long* (Alfred A. nopfs, 1969), p. 753.

[21] *Chicago Sun Times*, 8-21-68.

[22] Harold D. Lasswell and Abraham Kaplan, *Power and Society* (Yale University Press, 1950), p. 262.

[23] Banfield, *Political Influence*, pp. 251–2.

[24] Dahl, *Who Governs*, pp. 188–9.

[25] Dahl, *Who Governs*, p. 139 (emphasis added).

[26] *Ibid.*, p. 119.

[27] *Ibid.*, pp. 136–7.

[28] Sabonjian changed from the Democratic to the Republican label when running for his fourth term as mayor.

[29] Sayre and Kaufman, p. 225.

[30] Tugwell, p. 467.

[31] Banfield, *Political Influence*, Chapter 5.

[82] Edward Banfield and James Q. Wilson, *City Politics* (Vintage, 1963), p. 109.

[83] Moses, pp. 12–14.

[84] V. O. Key, p. 62.

[85] *Ibid.,* p. 46.

[86] Sayre and Kaufman, p. 669.

5

On the Nature of Political Trust

Many of the office transactions observed during this study are forms of political activity that normally attract little more than historical coverage as remnants of a dying variety of politics—the political machine. Presumably the modern political executive juggles programs and policies—not the personal problems of constituents. He examines proposed action in an effort to find programs which are acceptable to a constituency which is increasingly middle-class and increasingly dominated by the doctrines of good government politics. Government by patronage and friendship is struggling with few weapons and decreasing numbers against the large and powerful forces which demand progressive (non-machine) government and attention to the "public"—not the "private" interest.

Yet Waukegan can hardly be seen as a city of the poor or the foreign, and the mayor operates independently of party machinery. When a politician in the "post-machine" era achieves such remarkable success by incorporating tactics so suspiciously old fashioned, one must inquire into his reasons and ask if there aren' perhaps persistent elements in American politics that have been slighted in the too neat categorizations: machine and good government, old and new.

If these observations can be generalized to other political systems, far too little attention is paid to the importance the politician gives, if only in terms of time and energy, to creating and maintaining a good "image," eliciting and holding the trust and confidence of his constituents and those with whom he must work, maintaining needed communication with those who can tell him the success of his maneuverings in the eyes of his colleagues and his constituents.

In discussing his reasons for allotting his time as he does, for behaving as he does in various situations, and for taking the stands he does when controversy breaks out, Sabonjian mentioned the need for *creating or maintaining trust* more often than any other consideration. He keeps an open office door and attends civic, ethnic, social and religious functions because "It's necessary in order to build people's confidence in you. They have to know that you are their representative, that you're *not* too busy to care about them, that you can be trusted." He gives priority to the requests of subleaders because "Nobody would trust a guy who wasn't loyal to his friends." He refused to act on urban renewal for fear that "They would have thought I was working for the merchants."

Trust is essential in dealings with both constituents and participants. American politicians are always candidates dependent upon constituent favor. Elections are too frequent to allow "electability" ever to slip far from the politician's mind. All notions of centralization of influence by a political executive assume his incumbence in office. Yet little attention is paid to the effects of perpetual candidacy on his role. One consequence is the limitation of action to projects which have predictable, popular, short-run results. This proposition can be easily deduced from the developed model of the political entrepreneurs if the frequency of elections is considered as a factor.

The manipulation of influence for the realization of projects which will, in the judgment of the politician, ingratiate more voters than it will alienate, or at least prevent action objectionable to any significant interest, is a valid way of viewing office security. Nevertheless, in the view of Robert Sabonjian, far more is involved. He sees a need for trust, which accounts for much of the 'old-fashioned' behavior he includes in his daily relations as well as his role in controversies.

In addition to the problems of perpetual candidacy, there is the problem of relying on informal dealings in relations with participants. In informal systems, exchanges are not explicit, formal safeguards are absent, and there are time lapses between favor and assumed return. Peter Blau notes that: "Since there is no way to assure an appropriate return for a favor, social exchange requires trusting others to discharge their obligations."[1] Thus in the actual operation of a system of informal exchange as well as in its overt image, trust is essential.

In the same way, the ability to coordinate exchanges between or among individuals and groups requires trust. As Sabonjian says of his union-management arbitration in local industry strikes: "They can't talk straight to one another where they can to a guy in the middle that they trust. That's why I'm proud of my negotiations. I've been able to elicit the trust of both management and labor." As in the case of program selection, pure logic can be used to deduce the politician's need to create trust—if cultural as well as constitutional prescriptions are considered among the basic premises of action.

An American politician must expend enormous energy, whether he is campaigning or in office, in an uphill battle merely to justify his profession, let alone his right to snatch or inveigle the use of additional resources in order to centralize influence in himself.[2] Indeed the formal fragmentation of authority which necessitates informal centralization of influence was the purposive creation of a people who, distrustful of political power, intended its balance and limitation. Arnold Rose quotes a defeated candidate for congress:

> My impression was that some of the hostile and apathetic reactions were not personal to me or to Democrats in general but rather to politicians as such. To these persons politics appeared to represent frustration and futility. They seemed to feel that nothing good can come of politics, that much of their troubles and perplexity is caused by acts and omissions of government, and that they would rather not be reminded of this painful and mysterious fact about which they feel they can do nothing.[3]

Robert Dahl looks toward the underlying norms which produce distrust of politicians (dealers in power) when he examines the "opportunity costs" mitigating against full exploitation of power resources—by anyone.

> . . . part of the explanation lies in beliefs widely endorsed in liberal societies which stress the essentially immoral quality of 'power' by people over other people. These norms seem to be both specific and general: They specifically single out power over others as evil except under certain conditions, and unlimited power over others as always evil. . . . In the United States, certainly, a number of different institutions, including the family and schools, stress the propriety of maintaining a rough equality of influence in one's relations with one another; often the norms even seem to place heavy influence on avoiding influence entirely.[4]

Dispersal of governmental authority as a means of controlling the power of politicians is, then, both a constitutional fact and a cultural norm. The politician who wishes to centralize power in himself through informal mechanisms must do so in a culture which purposely did not give him that formal authority and which requires his frequent reappearance before voters. To engage in constitutionally questionable dealings in a society where one is dependent for position and ability to act upon a population already suspicious of the political enterprise and committed to the control of the politician's activities is indeed a formidable undertaking. Yet to fail to act, to accept the immobilizing restrictions of the constitutional framework, is to produce inaction and allow slack— thus the opportunity for enterprising opposition. While the American politician must deal with the cultural distrust which surrounds political power, he must also appreciate American impatience and the penchant of Americans for action and accomplishment.

Norton Long describes the two-fold requirements of government, arising from this political dilemma.

> Two things are necessary for the well disciplined government of any considerable territory: a generally accepted ideology creating centripetal symbols of legitimacy, and a bureaucracy to provide a controlled instrument both for the exercise of power and the authoritative interpretation of the ideology.[5]

Although Long is talking about government of a larger scale and consequently proposes the political party and a legitimating ideology as mechanisms responsive to these needs, the needs themselves seem quite aptly those of any government, or at least any government over a heterogeneous population.

Banfield and Dahl focus on the creation of the bureaucracy; little attention is paid anywhere in the literature to the mechanisms of legitimation which make its operation possible. Interestingly, while Banfield is not concerned with the legitimation of the informal centralization he describes, the alternatives he proposes for government action are in fact derivatives of the classical Weberian typology of legitimate forms of power. Charismatic, or what Banfield calls "personality" politics, is a means of centralizing influence through the capturing of a mass following. This is the alternative he sees as likely for a society such as the United States where power decentralization is both a value and a constitutional provision. The remaining alternatives implied in Banfield's discussion are those that result when one of the above restrictions does not hold. In London, he says, decentralization is not a value. While the power of the city council leader, like that of the American mayor, is extra-legal, it is not informal. "There are explicit understandings which give him a right to issue orders; consequently he need not 'buy' control in the Chicago manner." In contradistinction to this London variety of "traditional" authority is the situation in which the constitution provides for sufficient power centralization. In such a case the political head would have "formal authority commensurate with the requirements of the tasks he undertakes;" so that "he would not have to engage in this kind of undertaking."[6]

The entrepreneurial centralization of influence must be legitimated in practice. It could not be an effective means of coordination if it were not in some way legitimated and the need for legitimacy is one of the most important considerations determining the role of the political entrepreneur.

Talcott Parsons suggests two ways in which this legitimation is accomplished. Comparing systems of power and influence to economic systems, he says that, like money, power and influence must be seen as symbols of exchange which are effective only so long as they are accepted as legitimate. He refers to this necessary acceptance as "the problem of trust."[7]

The first type of legitimation (which Parsons associates with power) is deduced from the effectiveness of collective action for the purposes of the individual. One will entrust his security to a system of power if he "has confidence that his expectations will be effectively fulfilled through agencies beyond his personal control, because the power 'system' is effective." Effectiveness, in turn, is dependent upon backing by real assets (ability to coerce compliance), institutionalized norms surrounding authority, and legitimation (acceptance) of the power of leadership elements.[8]

The second type of trust (which Parsons associates with influence) is related not to the operating effectiveness of a system but to unverified trust in communications from leaders. "The crucial thing to look for seems to be a symbolic act or component of action on ego's [person influencing] part which communicates a generalized intention on the basis of which trust in more specific intentions is requested and expected."[9]

Insofar as Banfield and Dahl address the problem of legitimation, they do so in terms of attempts on the part of the politician to create a facade by means of which centralized direction is defined in terms of technical logic or democratic decision. Banfield leans toward the first.

> Since he takes and uses authority which the constitution-makers intended to put beyond his reach, the political head is frequently excoriated in the press and elsewhere as an enemy of democracy. He is told he ought to be ashamed of himself for being a boss, although the system of government could not possibly do the things the critics want done unless the decentralization of authority were somehow overcome. He must, therefore, boss while pretending not to.[10]

Thus Banfield's political head goes to great lengths to present his administration as a "force for clean and progressive government."[11] He does this by sponsoring programs which will create the appropriate image and by recruiting civic leaders to act as intermediaries to deal with the press, the civic associations, and the public generally. A paramount function of the co-opted civic leader is:

> to legitimate the plans of the political head. In Chicago, politicians are regarded with distrust and career civil servants with mild contempt. If official acts are to have the confidence of the public, they must be approved by laymen whose competence and disinterestedness are considered to be beyond question.[12]

Dahl discusses the use of democratic rituals to disguise the nature of official decision.

> . . . the American creed of democracy and equality prescribes many forms and procedures from which the actual practices of leaders diverge. Consequently to gain legitimacy for their actions leaders frequently surround their covert behavior with democratic rituals. These rituals . . . serve to disguise reality. . . .[13]

Thus Dahl tells us that "in a country like the United States where there is a strong democratic ethos" the tasks of subleaders not only include aid in strategy and policy formation and the carrying out of dull, time consuming and highly specialized work, but "helping by their very existence to furnish legitimacy to the actions of the leaders by providing a democratc facade."[14] Similarly in making up the party slates

. . . the whole paraphernalia of democratic procedures is employed
not so much to insure control from below as to give legitimacy and
acceptability to the candidates selected by the leaders.[15]

And the functions of the Citizens' Action Commission in the urban
redevelopment program

seem to have been roughly equivalent to those performed by the
democratic rituals of the political parties in making nominations for
public office; citizen participation gave legitimacy and acceptability
to the decisions of the leaders. . . .[16]

The notion of overt conformity with the traditions of the political
culture is not a new one. Machiavelli notes in *Discourses* that

He who desires or attempts to reform the government of the state,
and wishes to have it accepted and capable of maintaining itself to
the satisfaction of everybody, must at least retain the semblance of
old forms; so that it may seem to the people that there has been no
change in the institutions, even though in fact they are entirely
different from the old ones. For the majority of mankind are satisfied with appearances, as though they were realities, and are often
even more influenced by the things that seem than by those that
are.[17]

I think Machiavelli would accept the word "change" where he
uses "reform." If so, informal centralization of influence constitutes a "change" from the formal prescriptions of the democratic
process.

In summation, Banfield and Dahl see legitimation of the system
in terms of the politician's concealing or disguising the degree of
centralization which in fact underlies executive decision. Such
tactics are logical answers to the definitions these men pose of the
executive role. Banfield argues that a Chicago political head sees
himself as "chairman of a discussion group."[18] Dahl's politicians
see themselves as bound by a set of widely held assumptions which
require their game to be played within the vague dictates of the
"democratic creed."[19]

Although Sabonjian appreciates and uses these strategie he
more often assumes an approach based on another notion of the
executive role. As Sabonjian sees it, his job is not so much to safe-
guard the democratic process as to represent the community's
largest constituency—that body which elected him—in the administration of governmental affairs. Most consistently he works

to demonstrate the appropriateness of his handling the business of the community on behalf of the community; he does not emphasize the technical or democratic processes underlying administrative decision. His strategy is to seek the trust of the city's diverse groups, i.e. convince them through promise and product that their interests are safe with and well-represented by his administration. Sabonjian is far less concerned with maintaining a democratic facade than with the electoral affirmation he has come to expect. He told a newly elected council:

> You will find me more than fair. But I also say this: If we're going to play games, I'm prepared for games too. . . . I do not intend to sit here and waste the time of the city or my time, playing games, fighting hidden enemies or personality questions only. . . .
>
> When the council votes on a controversial issue they say the mayor has so many votes. I think the people of Waukegan have so many votes—they elected me.

In the literature, notions of representation are commonly associated with the role of the leader as opposed to say the boss or the office-holder. Lasswell and Kaplan state:

> The leader acts as representative of the group, and other groups and leaders react to him in that perspective. Symbols of identification make the relationship explicit. The leader acts in the name of the group; the group sees in him what Michels describes as "a magnified image of their own ego." The identification is thereby sentimentalized: the group is loyal to the leader. Thus leadership may be concisely characterized as the exercise of power with respect and loyalty from the domain.[20]

These authors see leadership (the exercise of power with respect and loyalty from the domain) as existing when a group perceives the embodiment of its ideal norms in an individual.

This is similar to the position of George Homans who states that "the leader must live up to the norms of the group—all the norms of the group—better than any follower."[21] "Any failure on the part of the leader to live up to the group norms undermines his social rank and hence the presumption that his orders are to be obeyed."[22] Although the orders he issues must be within reason, the ability of the leader to take the initiative for the group (to function as leader) in directing the "moving equilibrium" requires that group members allow him the benefit of the doubt in obeying orders. That is, the members must be willing to obey an order while waiting to see if the results will be acceptable.[23] For Homans, this is a function of the leader's social rank within the group.

Sabonjian seeks to establish the kind of trust which will allow him the benefit of the doubt in making decisions for the community. But the ability of the politician to portray himself as the embodiment of group norms, as the group's *natural* leader, is only one way of acquiring the respect and loyalty which legitimate dominance. *Effective* leadership can be based on other types of trust. Indeed of the various types of trust, the appeal to commonality with the group or its norms is probably the most limited. It is limited first because of the negative image the office-holder inherits. This is not necessarily countered by expressions of commonality or virtue, although they may help. It is limited, second, because the executive faces Herculean problems in finding a common denominator which is not so common as to be possessed by all his opponents.

Robert Moses and Fiorello La Guardia seem to have shared Sabonjian's definition of the executive role as the exercise of effective leadership. In addition, the two shared the view that acquiring the ability to exercise effective leadership (as defined by the individual politician) may require tactics which are not implied in the notion of natural leadership. The latter implies a consciousness of kind and purpose on the part of the group which the politician would lead. The other types of trust do not.

Moses remarks:

It must be admitted that in exploiting racial and religious prejudices LaGuardia could run circles around the bosses he despised and derided. When it came to raking ashes of the Old World hates, warming ancient grudges, waving the bloody shirt, tuning the ear to ancestral voices, he could out-demagogue the demagogues. And for what purpose? To redress old wrongs abroad? To combat foreign levy or malice domestic? To produce peace on the Danube, the Nile, the Jordan? Not on your tintype. Fiorello LaGuardia knew better. . . .

. . . he was too shrewd, too honest, too basically cool, too calculating, too essentially American to believe his own occasional lapses into political claptrap. *Why, then, did he use the familiar rabble-rousing technique? He did it to get and stay elected. It was the price he paid for the opportunity to provide as good government as the people would stand for,* and in the process he learned that, given time, the voters are smarter than the politicians and much readier for independent government. Otherwise Fiorello LaGuardia would not have been mayor three terms.[24]

Greer addressed this problem in his study of labor leaders.

. . . the leader faces a conflict between his personal position as an administrator and democratic processes. . . . His work is highly specialized and requires a wide range of uncommon skills, yet his tenure in office is at the mercy of elections. These, in turn, are at the mercy of a membership which does not fully understand his work, the union's situation or the resulting commitments. . . .

In reconciling his own managerial position with his member's subordinate place in industry, he uses many tactics. He plays the role of the ordinary member in those organizational interstices where this is possible. His vocabulary and syntax, his personal appearances and interests, include those common to his members. He makes a point of personalizing relations with as many members as possible: he tries to be available in person.[25]

If the "democratic" leader can assume (as La Guardia and the union officials did) that (1) the best interests of his organization (New York City or a union local) are his primary concern and (2) he is better able to achieve the group's goals using his own techniques than he is using those formally provided, he can justify to himself (and ultimately, if his assumptions are accurate, to others) the behavior he feels is necessary to get and stay elected and at the same time do his job.

Arnold Rose describes the politician's ability to play these dual roles in terms of his ability to "objectify himself," to create a "third person image."[26] Such objectification makes it possible for the politician to work at one level towards creating the trust he needs to proceed at another level with governing on behalf of the group.

According to the secretary who worked for both Sabonjian and his predecessor, the earlier mayor protected himself by staying clearly within the bounds of constitutional legality and bureaucratic limits. She compared him with Sabonjian—

Coulson [former mayor] was a lawyer, Sabonjian is a businessman. Where Coulson accepted red tape and worked within it and through it, Bob [Sabonjian] says, "This is what we're going to do and this is how." He cuts red tape when it gets in the way of what he wants to do. Coulson cared more about procedure. Sabonjian is more concerned with getting things done.

Sabonjian's strategy is to convince the diverse elements in the community that he is their trustworthy executor. He may then proceed with the practical business of governing unhampered by bureaucratic detail and bulwarks of citizen participation.

When one correctly perceives goals and, by shortcutting procedural handicaps, achieves them, he has maximized gains because contrary to the good government emphasis on procedural propriety, many Americans feel that ends do indeed justify means. Often it is only when goals become objectionable that means are called seriously into question. (Lyndon Johnson's power was not questioned until after Viet Nam.) Again quoting Moses:

> . . . Herbert Bayard Swope once remarked, "I don't have any formula for success, but I know the sure formula for failure—try to please everybody." In the ultimate sense of enduring reputation H. B. S. was probably right, but most American statesmen have been pretty successful in applying the sure formula for failure. La-Guardia was one of those extraordinary men who had it both ways— that is, he lived by the practical rules of American politics and was also above them.[27]

Such phenomena occur because some politicians are able to work at two levels. They are able to acquire such trust among their constituents that the means by which ends are achieved are not questioned. Thus they are able to centralize enough power to achieve goals while retaining legitimacy.

Sabonjian seeks this status. Like La Guardia, he seeks the "opportunity to provide as good government as the people will stand for." He feels that the trust of his constituents and his work partners is the critical condition underlying his ability to work toward the goals the majority seeks but without centralization could not achieve, or toward the goals he is sure the public may not recognize as needed but will applaud when realized. It also provides a backstop to recrimination in the event of program failure and thus increases his freedom to act. It is essential to recognize the interplay between the limits which the requirements of trust impose upon executive action and the extensions which trust (for whatever reason conferred) allows executive action.

The process whereby the politician creates a mandate is, in a sense, like the process whereby he centralizes bureaucratic control. Just as the politician who begins with inadequate formal powers may use the powers he does possess as initial capital in acquiring further powers, the politician who begins with inadequate cultural legitimacy may use those definitions which do confer authority in acquiring further legitimacy. While cultural definition by and large mitigates against political trust, the politician seeks those points where he sees an opportunity to create a contrary impression.

SUMMARY

Sabonjian considers the business of creating trust to be of first priority. By increasing trust, he increases his directive potential. He assures his own security in office and improves his ability to gain cooperation. He makes opposition more costly and undercuts its ability to gain support. He frees himself from perpetual review, increases his independence, and multiplies his effectiveness in securing goals.

Sabonjian works to establish trust in himself in order that he may proceed with the business of running Waukegan—as executive director, not as chairman of a political discussion group whose members possess constitutional checks on one another and whose collective achievement is apt to be inaction. An executive, he feels, will not be called to account for centralization of effective power so long as constituents believe that power is being exercised in their best interests. The constituents—who return Sabonjian to office with such resounding margins, elect his endorsed candidates, and approve his programs—seem to agree.

TYPES OF POLITICAL TRUST

Trust is an implicit requisite of executive success. The last section noted the logic of this position and the importance attached to it by Sabonjian. The building and maintaining of trust is a constant and indeed overriding consideration in his mayoral decisions. It conditions his behavior regarding specific directive or integrative goals; it is also a specific goal of action, a useful political resource sought independently of other goals.

In discussing the commitments to which the mayor must attend, two overlapping variables emerged. First, *participation* in politics. Persons who were repeatedly and systematically involved, were called political actors. Persons who were occasionally or never involved (except as voters), were called constituents. The former group had direct channels of communication with government officials. The latter had only indirect relations with these persons; their awareness was necessarily based on observables—sporadic encounters with officials, visible actions and products, associate reports, and media images.

Direct observations from the mayor's office brought out a variant of this classification. Once again, political actors and constituents were distinguished. However, the view of constituents which emerged from these data was restricted to that changing body of constituents who were engaged in direct (if sporadic and unsystematic) communication with the mayor. Except for reports by these persons on the views or needs of other constituents, the data emphasized relations with that group of constituents which engaged in person-to-person relations with the mayor. These rotating representatives of the larger category were called "clients."

In discussing trust, both variables are appropriate: the nature of participation (systematic, non-systematic), and the nature of communication (direct, indirect). Clients constitute the category of overlap: non-systematic, but direct. In this section, the terms actors and constituents will be used, but constituents will consist both of clients, who come into direct contact with the mayor, and of observers, whose image of him is limited to indirect information. Both categories of constituents are, of course, capable of becoming political actors.

Participation	Communication
Systematic (Actors)	Political Actors — Direct
Non-systematic (Constituents)	Clients / Observers — Indirect

Although the relationship is far from perfect, I feel there is a rough correspondence between the degree of autonomy enjoyed by particular persons or groups and the grounds upon which they will determine trustworthiness. Persons with limited resources may feel more dependent upon personal relations than are persons with a greater number of alternatives. This might contribute to a tendency to trust primary human relations with officials. Persons with somewhat greater resources (group membership, occupational skill, home investment) are increasingly apt to see these resources as foci of identification and values to be protected by "representatives." Individuals whose occupation, income or education allow (or even require) them to view events from a broad institutional perspective seem to trust the actions of persons who are acting in awareness of these forces. Thus the three categories of trust with which I shall be concerned are:

1. Trust in a primary relation
2. Trust in value representation
3. Trust in role adequacy

Trust in a Primary Relation   Talcott Parsons, in his discussion of influence, asks if there is an intrinsic source of persuasion which above all others "has special likelihood of inspiring trust?" His answer is this:

> If . . . we remember that we are dealing specifically with social interaction, it seems reasonable to suggest that the most favorable condition under which alter will trust ego's efforts to persuade him (independent of specific factors or "inherently" trustworthy intentions) will be when the two stand in a mutual relation of diffuse solidarity, when they belong together in a collectivity on such a basis that, so long as the tie holds, ego *could not* have an interest in trying to deceive alter. We may then suggest that common belongingness in a *Gemeinschaft* type of solidarity is the primary "basis" of mutual influence.[28]

According to Parsons, *Gemeinschaft* associations should be sufficient to assure trust without the need of concrete information or binding contracts (specific intentions may be inferred from generalized intentions).

Trust in a primary relationship, refers to the kind of trust (whether or not it is the "primary basis of mutual influence") which is associated with solidarity—with *Gemeinschaft* society, with family, and with friendship. In such relationships, the social unit is central. Within the group, there is recognized membership, personal status, and individual significance. Expectations and reactions occur in terms of concern, understanding, and affect.

Product is secondary; competitive behavior is eliminated by definition.

Sabonjian tries to infuse his political dealings with the qualities associated with the *Gemeinschaft* relationship by demonstrating concern for individuals and for the groups with which they identify, and by attending to particularistic cases and to the integration of the social unit. He extends recognition and significance. He mediates between the individual and the larger order.

Most of the mayor's efforts to personalize relationships can be read as efforts to create trust through the creation of primary group orientations. At the same time, it is possible to think of the leader of a group, if he be really this (or aspires to be this), as occupying a more important position in the group. Sebastian de Grazia feels we have paid too little attention to the leader's role in maintaining the very belief systems which bind the group together. He defines belief systems as the basic denominator of citizens which "expresses their ideas concerning their relationship to one another and to their rulers."[29] Drawing heavily on anthropological and historical data, de Grazia argues that the leader in the political community is the person responsible for providing and protecting his people with regard to these basic belief systems:

> More scholarly regard should be given to the central role of the ruler in the political ideology. Men will quietly abide in their systems of belief so long as they feel that all their values are assured by their ruling entity.[30]
>
> One finds that the deterioration of beliefs follows fast on any revelation that the reigning 'ruler' is either unable or unwilling to perform his commitments.[31]

The leader's part in assuring such values is apt to require very concrete associations with his following—including both physical proximity and symbolic presence. De Grazia refers on this point to Gaetano Mosca's *The Ruling Class*. In this book, Mosca discusses the change that occurred in the medieval relationship between the Polish nobles and the serfs.

> . . . the Polish nobles in the Middle Ages levied almost all the produce of their serfs, beat them, chose the most buxom of their daughters for their households and otherwise "exploited" them. . . .

Yet the serfs did not rebel against the lord,

so long as he remained with them, spoke their language, swore the same oaths, ate the same kind of food, wore the same style of clothes, exhibited the same manners or lack of them, had the same rustic superstitions. But from the time when he adopted the French ruffled dress and minced speech, gave luxurious balls after the manner of Versailles and tried to dance the minuet, "peasantry and nobility became two peoples apart." The serfs grew reluctant to support him, [and] revolted periodically and viciously, despite the fact that part of their lord's newly acquired French education was a "more humane" treatment of his subjects. . . .

de Grazia explains this change as a loss of solidary trust. The Polish dissidence arose from:

a string of circumstances which convinced the members of the community (in this case the serfs) that the lord to whom they paid homage no longer made their commonweal his primary concern. In other words, they felt that he had deserted them and that they could no longer rely on him to protect them from enemies, defend their faith, and represent them to God.[32]

This sentiment is noted by Lasswell and Kaplan also. They say:

. . . authority cannot hold itsef so far distant from its domain as to strain identifications or otherwise weaken solidarity; and, of course, the exercise of authority necessarily involves some degree of contact with those over whom it is being exercised. Machiavelli advises the Prince to minimize distance in a literal sense—to reside in newly acquired territories, so as to strengthen loyalty to and respect for the new authority. More commonly, authority relies on symbols to make possible "action at a distance." Either he acts through representatives, to whom partial authority has been delegated, or his direct contacts are formalized by ritualistic and other symbols.[33]

These authors are stressing interrelationships and interdependencies more than commonalities—a sense of belongingness in a group and an identification of that group with its leader. It is these points which are relevant to the mayor's role in a community. While local government may appear trivial to community residents, the locality is the focus of the primary relationships (family, ethnic group, and neighborhood) which bind persons together, and it is the primary relationships which mediate between the individual and the outside or secondary structures. Although there is a tendency for kin or fictive kin ties to be stronger in low autonomy areas, they play an important role in the lives of the more autonomous as well.[34] It is easy to see how a politician might preserve a notion of commonality with those who shared common origins. By continuing old associations and living habits, he might prevent the kind of separation which Mosca says defeated the Polish nobility.

The question now is the extent to which *Gemeinschaft* trust might be elicited from persons in the community whose natural identifications would not produce allegiance to or trust in a particular leader. The Lasswell and Kaplan quotation above shows that Machiavelli had concerned himself with this problem and advised rulers to move into and reside in acquired territories in order that distance between ruler and ruled might be minimized loyalty and respect increased.

The first step in creating *Gemeinschaft* trust, one might conclude, is the reduction of distance and the destroying of indifference. Reduction of distance, as these authors have used it, can be interpreted as an increase in accessibility—a movement toward the primary and away from the secondary relationship. One way to effect this movement would be to create another primary community in which the segmented groups might all belong. Conceivably, one might create a new sense of "place," of "roots," and of commonality—a new community which could provide an alternative to old allegiances or could occur concomitant with them.

Sabonjian tries to create such a *Gemeinschaft* trust. His emphasis on social integration to maximize output, minimize organization along competitive lines, and prevent conflict goes along with the building of trust. There are many ways the trust aspect is emphasized in both person-to-person relations (with actors and with clients) and in projected images.

> The city's top executive told his audience that he had no plan to improve racial and ethnic relations within the Waukegan area except to work harder, create more friendship, and "learn to trust each other." (3-13-69)

This preceded a statement quoted earlier: "The city can't do it all. You are the city. The people have to do something." In these statements the need for social and productive integration for community identification, and for trust among brothers (including the mayor) are simultaneous pleas.

Other means of creating a collective identity are lighter, but important. Sabonjian uses the media and his public presence to create a symbolic unity. He talks in general terms about his pride in Waukegan and the pride of its citizens, and he works to make it a place to be proud of. The mere assumption that there is a collective body of persons who consider themselves to be "Waukeganites" may be a tool in this effort. Sabonjian's assumption appears less remarkable when one realizes that Mayor Daley goes so far as to assume that there is a collective body of persons called Chicagoans, indeed a collective body of persons so identified with Chicago and with one another that they are capable of feeling a collective insult. In a response to an attack on Chicago, Daley said: "We've been listening to statements from outsiders for a long time and I think the people of Chicago are about filled up with these kind of statements."[33]

That Sabonjian sees Waukegan as a place among places, came forth vividly to those who attended the International Fellowship Fair which was held in Waukegan in 1967. Ethnic groups were invited to display ethnic art and national costumes, to hand out literature, and to perform traditional dances and music. A large number of ethnic groups was represented at the event. All partitions separating the high school gymnasiums were removed to provide the festival with the equivalent space of four gymnasiums. Booths lined all walls. Ethnic dances were performed in the center. Visitors could see the wares of nationality groups from around the world. But first in line as one started the tour of these exhibits was the mayor's "Waukegan Booth," complete with the mayor. City awards and souvenirs could be seen along with pictures of city officials, city heroes and famous visitors. The city flag (something Sabonjian had decided should exist) was there too.[36] Indeed the mayor had emptied an office filled with the mementos of his tenure and the legends of the city to bring them to this festival. At first this booth seemed inappropriate. Yet the appreciation of visitors was clear, as was their renewed identification with the city. Time and time again persons mentioned how grateful they were the mayor was able to bring to them these symbols of and reports on their city—since "It is so hard to get down to City Hall to see them."

The city as place has many other aspects. It consists, for example, of common knowledge and common backgrounds. Sabonjian emphasizes widely shared referents when possible. He named a street after a thirty-two year alderman and declared a local holiday to recognize a teacher who through the years had taught a very large portion of locally born Waukeganites. Such behavior is intended to shrink city size and reduce the perceived distance between citizen and city official.

City heroes are another shared value and a symbol of city as place. The heroes mentioned in the mayor's earlier quoted letter to the Chicago disc jockey were portrayed as representatives of the *city*. For Jack Benny's 1968 birthday, Sabonjian sent the former Waukeganite a giant greeting card with best wishes "From your friends in Waukegan" (2-14-68). The newspaper printed a large picture of Sabonjian holding the opened card to show the collective signature. Sabonjian made arrangements for Waukegan's Jack Benny to be present at the 1959 Centennial and he arranged for the comedian to appear at the Waukegan celebration of the Illinois Sesquecentennial. On the latter occasion, full page newspaper pictures showed Sabonjian playing straight man for Benny in a film which would be sent to Springfield for showing at the state celebration.

When Waukeganite Pat Nugent married President Johnson's daughter, Luci, Sabonjian's present to the couple was a painting by a local artist portraying a Waukegan park. He sent a bell representing Waukegan to a bell ringing program in San Diego, California. Every out-of-town visitor who appears at the mayor's city hall office receives a cordial welcome from the mayor and leaves with a copy of the League of Women Voters book telling about the city, a glass replica of the Waukegan lighthouse, and an ashtray imprinted with "Waukegan, Illinois." When John Kennedy was assassinated, Sabonjian arranged for the production and distribution of a 33rpm record entitled "Waukegan's Tribute to JFK." The record featured the Great Lakes Navy Band and other local contributors. Such maneuverings may be indirect ways of attracting money-bringing conventions, business, and industries to the city. They may enhance Sabonjian's chances for higher political office. Their importance for internal consumption is, however, critical. Sabonjian is making Waukegan "a place to be proud of," a place acquaintances have heard of, a place to which conventions and industries come, and a place with which citizens will identify.

Moreover, in creating, assuming, implying, or imagining that there is *a* Waukegan, he is creating for himself the possibility of a particular type of leadership role. It is that type of role which is appropriate to the leader of a solidary group. If he is able to convince others of *his* identification with the "city" (whether or not they internalize this notion of community), he is able to imply *Gemeinschaft* solidarity with everyone at once. In doing so, he hopes to project the notion that, as Parsons phrased it, "they belong together in a collectivity on such a basis that, so long as the tie holds, ego could not have an interest in trying to deceive alter."

The first element in this leadership role is, as Machiavelli suggested, accessibility to all. With rare exceptions the mayor takes all phone calls personally. "People get mad or get their feelings hurt," he said, "if they can't talk to the mayor personally."

The fact that psychological as well as physical accessibility is important is reflected in the following remarks:

Richard Daley:
I don't hear much about what is going on around the country. I'm strictly a local boy serving the great city of Chicago and the state of Illinois.[37]

Robert Sabonjian, on the Viet Nam war:
I don't know much about it. I'll leave that stuff to you people with the college educations.

Richard Daley:
Please don't write anything like that. I'm not better than anyone else. I don't want to look like a fellow who tells other people what to do.[38]

Robert Sabonjian:
I can't do that. I'd look like a dictator.

There is another aspect, however, to the *Gemeinschaft* leader. The leader in the solidary group is more than simply accessible to the group; he is responsible for it. Trust in the mode of relationship allows persons to opt out of active lobbying for their interests, which are instead assumed to be the concern of the leader. In this sense, primary trust in a *Gemeinschaft* leader is associated with low political awareness among followers (deriving either from a lack of sophistication about politics or a lack of interest— given the assumptions). While this type of trust is sought from all persons, it is achieved most often among low autonomy persons. The security of such persons in a little understood world is most confidently achieved through attachment to a trusted leader who, it is believed, can and will tend to the group's welfare. In a statement promoting this type of relationship Mayor Daley remarked:

> The old bosses were not interested in what was good for the public welfare. They were interested only in what was good for themselves. The new objective of leadership is not what you can do for yourself, but what you can do for the people.[39]

The notion of a leader who is concerned and responsible for his people is more easily specified if one examines a community which in fact resembles the true *Gemeinschaft* model. The Puerto Rican community in Waukegan is a very solid community, indeed a community which can still produce a directed vote. A squabble over the leadership of the community developed during this study of Waukegan. Some of it reached the mayor's office. Three incidents are indicative. The first occurred when the community's established leader was visiting Puerto Rico. A counter group proposed for alderman a candidate who had not been endorsed by the regular leader. The mayor refused support, directing the following remark to a man who had apparently vied some years ago for the now challenged leadership position in the Puerto Rican community.

> You are a Goddamn Judas. You've got this chip on your shoulder because you lost your power to Eddy. But that was your fault, not his. If you're going to be President [of the Puerto Rican Society] you've got to be a strong president. . . . You *let* that leadership slip away. Eddy had that store where the people could meet. What did you ever do to be a leader? As a matter of fact, what did you ever do for the Puerto Ricans, period? Who gave thousands and thousands of dollars credit on groceries, who established the credit union, who established this contact with the mayor's office? Eddy, that's who.

The second episode occurred shortly after the first. The leader who had been under fire met with the mayor. Worried, Sabonjian pressed as to the seriousness of the division in the community.

> Sabonjian: If you think there's any chance that working [in the election] for ———— will hurt you, lay off.

Montano: They can't hurt me. They are only four men. There's no way they can hurt me. *My people* are with me. (emphasis added)

Sabonjian: Maybe it would be a good idea if you'd open some kind of a little store again where the people could congregate like they used to. So they could see you every day—

Montano: I know what I'm doing. They don't come to me now, but I go to them. . . .

The third incident occurred two years later when the Puerto Rican leader, solidly in place as leader, appeared in the office with one of the men who had been a member of the opposition group. The two had come on business unrelated to the long-ended feud, but they explained its end. "They didn't trust him," Montano said, speaking of the opposition leader. "He didn't care about the Puerto Ricans," the second man joined in. "He wanted to be *paid* for the work he did for the [Puerto Rican] Society. When the people found that out, they didn't want anything more to do with him."

Notions of concern for the group expressed through accessibility, selflessness, and performance are infused throughout these statements by Sabonjian, by a more genuinely *Gemeinschaft* leader, and by a follower. From these remarks one might predict a petty favor strategy, an open door, a wide attendance at community events, an insistence on efficient performance.

Explicit evidence of such a "patrón" role in Waukegan is found in all of these relationships between the mayor and actors, the mayor and clients, the mayor and the observing public. Newspaper accounts, while they refer to specific populations, registered also with the newspaper public. One article reports on actions by the mayor which express the analogy between the city and the community, the mayor and the patrón.

Mayor Robert Sabonjian said Tuesday the achievement of his administration of which he is proudest is the construction of housing for elderly citizens.

Sabonjian said elderly residents often can't afford to retire here, so they move away. "They've died of loneliness and heartbreak. They miss their grandchildren; they miss their children; they miss their friends."

"If a guy gets only $90 a month income, he can still live with dignity in his own hometown. He can rent an apartment here for $25–27 a month. . . ."

"Living here," he said, "they feel they're loved, they're part of their hometown. I think this is my greatest accomplishment—better than any overpasses, better than the expansion of the water plant, anything, because this is human need. This is compassion, this is love for the people who built this town who assumed all the responsibilities for building all the schools and things our children enjoy. This is the way to say 'thank you' to the people who carried the load." (4-2-69)

The article went on to tell about the mayor's summer job assistance given to 450 college students each year. Responding to criticism from the black community, he said, "I've got better than sixty colored kids in college right now." When job applications come from out-of-town students, they go to the end of the list. "Give the jobs to our own kids first."

Visual as well as verbal communication goes on between the mayor and his flock. One newspaper picture is particularly illustrative. A woman whose husband had died suddenly leaving her with four small children and no provision, discovered that the Loyal Order of Moose owned and maintained a home and school for the families of deceased members. She made arrangements to enter. A six inch square picture showed Sabonjian, a member of the Order, seeing the family off (4-9-68). Sabonjian was not mentioned in the article and seemingly had no personal connection with either the family or the charity—except as mayor of the hometown, seeing off townsmen.

A final incident concerns an opportunity which Sabonjian seized with enthusiasm and impetuosity. A terrible thunder and wind storm arrived in Waukegan on the deadline date for the purchase of Waukegan vehicle stickers. Sabonjian arrived at work nearly an hour earlier than usual; he entered the office running. His first call went to the radio station—his second to the newspaper. Sabonjian had extended the deadline until Monday. Citizens who could not "due to the severity of the weather" get downtown to purchase their stickers could get them Monday. They would not have to pay the penalty fee. The hundreds of persons who purchase their stickers on the last day knew they had a friend in City Hall. Having made his announcement Sabonjian went about his business, including his inquiry into the weather conditions

If Sabonjian seizes opportunities to project his identification and affiliation with persons in the community, he also avoids actions which might produce the opposite impression. When motives of self-aggrandizement could be imputed to action, Sabonjian is cautious. A developer offered Sabonjian a commission for a land transaction he had facilitated. Sabonjian said that, as mayor, he was anxious to get productive enterprises on usable property. "Get me a box of candy. I don't want any commission. If I started taking commissions I wouldn't be mayor very long."

A major political decision which appeared at first to be a confusing, if not contradictory move on the part of the mayor, in the end supplied supportive evidence for the importance of primary trust. At a meeting where Sabonjian and his closest advisors discussed strategies for the 1969 election, the question at issue was the mayor's change from the Democratic to the Republican Party. Behind the proposed change were several considerations. For many years, Sabonjian, a "bad" organization man, had not been getting along with leaders of the Democratic party. Since the riots in 1966, members of this body had been vocal in their criticism of the mayor. There was some question as to what kind of support would be forthcoming. Indeed the mayor believed party leaders might be his most serious opposition. If so, the party change made sense, for a small but organized and vociferous opposition would be apt to have a greater effect in the Democratic primary than in a citywide election. The change also made sense if the mayor intended to seek higher political office. As he approached his fourth term as mayor, this goal had begun to interest him. In the strongly Republican county and congressional district, the Democratic label was a loser. Winning at these levels would be easier as a Republican. Nomination for state office would also be easier. Having never been connected with the Democratic machine in Chicago, Sabonjian stood little chance of receiving a Democratic nomination for higher office. Republican politics were more open, and rich Lake County was influential in state politics. Arguing against the move was Sabonjian's concern (shared by several of his advisors) over the way in which the Democratic following—the loyal corps of stalwart supporters—would read the action. Would the "old-timers" think he had deserted them?

The mayor decided to run as an Independent, as he had in the Senate campaign. Running as an Independent would be consistent with the mayor's behavior and it would probably not appear to the old time ethnics that he had *left* the Democrats if he hadn't *become* a Republican. He could explain his taking the neutral label by pointing up his particular problems with the Democratic organization. When the paper announced the mayor's entry into the race, however, it was as a Republican. Sabonjian had changed strategy when he had learned of the legal difficulties involved in running on an Independent ticket. There are so many technicalities, he said, that he had been advised by legal council to run on an established party label. It was easy, he learned, for those interested in disqualifying a candidate, to invalidate an Independent ticket. He feared his determined and legalistic opposition might find such a technicality. On the other hand, he had launched a counter-offensive to offset the effects he had feared a party change would have on the trust of his south side core of support.

Sabonjian and his subleaders carried out a write-in campaign for the nomination of Sabonjian in the Democratic primary. The goal, as both he and his first captain told me, was not to win the nomination (although this nearly happened) but to assure the Democratic following that Bob was still one of them. As the subleader said, "The campaign to have Democrats write Bob in on the Democratic ballot has given them an out. They were disappointed sure, but now they can say: 'Bob must not have changed that much if he still wants our write-in votes as Democrats.'" The Sabonjian workers who had been canvassing the south side throughout the Sabonjian years went out once more to tell the old crowd the old story. The Republican newspaper publicized the unusual campaign including Sabonjian's assurances that he was not deserting his Democratic friends, and his pleas that they write his name in on their ballot.

Such techniques are used in projecting *Gemeinschaft* through the media or the intermediaries to the observers. The construct is similarly important in direct relations. Sabonjian talks of the importance of community goals in holding the trust of the political actors with whom he works, of not allowing the sincerity of his concern, his dependability or his honesty to be questioned. The *Gemeinschaft* type of trust is predominant among Sabonjian and his subleaders. Speaking of his insistence on cooperation from aldermen, the mayor made explicit his ideas:

. . . we work together. . . . You do something for them; they return the favor. I never ask for anything for myself though. I'd lose their confidence—only for the city. When you can show them something that's good for the city and it's a good thing and they believe it's a good thing because they have confidence that you want the best for the city—then you can work things out together. They won't trust you if they think you're in it for yourself.

Although the cases where independence is greater on the part of the persons with whom the mayor works are harder to classify, there is a personal aspect in the communication which forces a personal response. Wherever this can be inserted there is increased opportunity for gain. A great deal of freedom can be gained if constituents and cohorts believe implicitly that the man in charge has their welfare uppermost in mind.

This characteristic is frequently found in descriptions of powerful politicians:

> Mayor LaGuardia's instinct, like Governor Smith's was to welcome any idea that seemed to promise advantages to the public rather than to himself, an instinct which went far beyond ordinary decency, quick sympathy and the desire to redress wrongs. I don't mean that he was a sap or an easy mark or that he did not in the end figure out what this or that course of action would do to him, but this was not his primary or only concern. His impulses were generous and to a remarkable degree unselfish.[40]
>
> Moses commanded a great deal of deference because he made himself a model of an absolutely honest, tireless, devoted, and hugely effective civil servant.[41]
>
> Civic leaders—even those who were very critical of machine politicians—believed Ryan was honest, fair and well-intentioned. "Dan is a fine fellow," a Republican of an old Chicago family told an interviewer. . . . "He wants to do the right thing. I hate to oppose him."[42]

The reverse image has had negative effects. In spite of attempts to present a "folksy" image to the public, Lyndon Johnson's career was damaged by charges of "high-handedness," by what came to be known as the "credibility gap" and by the recurrent suggestion that there might exist a conflict between the interests of Lyndon Johnson and those of the public. Governor Stratton of Illinois suffered, in his relations with political actors, from a reputation of distance and questionable concern. A representative to the Illinois House stated that among his reasons for opposing a proposal by Governor Stratton was his feeling that the governor was a cold person. When the representative asked for something, he was sent to an assistant—without assurances that the assistant had orders to help him. "He liked a man who was warm, and who would do what he could to help you."[43]

In this study, cases where bonds of personal trust were created or came into play occurred very often between the mayor and the clientele portion of the constituency. Lower autonomy cases were more common than higher autonomy cases. Indirect information which constituents received from the media or from friends must have contributed to the specific approachability of the mayor. The notion in the political culture that the local official is a civil servant must have accounted for some general approachability. Whatever the source of the image, constituent initiation of direct interaction with the mayor provides a resource to the mayor in creating personal ties. Such initiated action provides the mayor with an opportunity to respond with help, with particularistic interest, with concern. It allows him to increase his secure support by including a greater number of relationships based on friendship. In direct interaction, he may extend individual significance and offer inclusion in the community he has created around himself.

Examples of letters which suggest a willingness to define the mayor as a particular type of powerful friend (accessible, concerned, sympathetic) are the following:

Dear Sir:

I know you are a very busy man and I do hate to take up any of your time; and when I do, I never get to talk all I want to, knowing you have more important things to care for makes me forget some of the things I want to say. I just hope you will find time to read this—[6 long pages]

Dear Mayor Sabonjian:

I'm writing this letter to you because I don't know anyone else to turn to. On Dec. 20, 1966, a young boy ran in to me. Demolished my car. I was in the hospital and I'm still paying Dr. bills. I had let my insurance lapse without knowing it. . . .

Mayor Robert Sabonjian

Mr. Mayor I know that you are a very influential man so I am writing to you. I am married and have one child and work for ———— in the Highland Park area. I would like your opinion of a company that pays their employees with a family and military

service $2.68 a hour and will hire what they call summer help at
$3.00 a hour right out of school. . . .

A letter from a teen suggests the mayor has projected personal
concern and responsibility.

> Dear Mayor Sabonjian,
>   I and my friends have a complaint to the city of Waukegan. We
> know you are trying to do your best of your ability to help the young
> people of your city. We would like you to do something about the
> bands down at the lake. . . . And there is something else I would
> like to know about the closing of Genesee Street [during trial Mall].
> . . . We all would like you to keep open the Street for there is
> nothing for young people to do on a Saturday night. . . .

When possible, Sabonjian responds to such overtures. The teen
received a four paragraph letter from the mayor regarding action
taken on the band problem, his concern about the lamentable
conflict between teens and businessmen, suggestions on how teens
might fill their time when bored, and thanks (twice mentioned)
for writing to him. The girl's letter had provided Sabonjian with
an opportunity. He could, in response to it, solidify into personal
status a relationship which had opened itself to this kind of communication. Such letters are common. Most get a personal response although "official" or "administrative" business is rarely
handled by mail—(it produced three letters during the summer).
    Sabonjian uses any interaction as an opportunity to create pri-
mary bonds of trust. A person applying for a liquor license is apt to
get unsolicited business advice. A girl employed by the library was
sent to the mayor's office on official business; before she left, she
had been quizzed by Sabonjian as to her salary, informed of the
mayor's rage at the low library salaries, and promised his attention
to the matter. A neutral letter from a west side black neighborhood was signed by thirty-four persons. The letter stated simply
that "The attached list of names has been taken to request sewer
repair and mosquito control. . . ." Thirty-four personal letters
went out (more than the entire remainder of the mayor's summer
correspondence).

> Dear ————:
>   I received your petition regarding sewer repair and mosquito con-
> trol. I have looked into the matter personally. By the time you re-
> ceive this letter action will have been taken to correct the problems.

I hope your situation is now improved. Feel free to contact my office if I can be of further assistance.

I remain

Your friend,

Sabonjian tries to personalize office business as well. He hopes persons who have come to see the mayor will leave having seen Bob Sabonjian. The following conversation, which occurred between Sabonjian and members of the NAACP, serves as an example.

NAACP spokesman:	I'd like you to meet S———, and T—— and D———. We were hoping to talk to you about the school board appointments.
Sabonjian:	I'm delighted you're here. Are you two guys brothers?
T———:	Yes, we are.
Spokesman:	We think that a major problem facing Waukegan schools is the unfamiliarity of some of the officials with the Waukegan situation. . . . We want to see people appointed to the board who will have the background for seeing Waukegan as a unit, who can look at the whole picture.
Sabonjian:	May I say something? What do you fellas do? T———, was it? And D———? And you're S———? I just want to know you a little better, that's all. You come in here and we right off start discussing business without getting acquainted at all. Where do you live? [Men give addresses] Say you live right over by me. Your wife isn't Sally?
J———:	Yes, she is.
Sabonjian (grinning):	Oh brother has she ever been a thorn in my side. Women just drive me nuts. I've got one on the school board, but I'll never make a mistake like that again. . . . They can never make up their minds. [Everybody laughs] Your wife and that damned employment agency. I'd be perfectly happy to work with her, but you tell her she's got to leave her chip at home.

J————:	Well, she's a very honest woman, and she'll tell you what she thinks.
Sabonjian:	I'll say she will. God. Now I feel like I know you a little better. You know what I mean? We can talk like friends. May I call you by your first names?

The school board appointments were discussed with Sabonjian and the forces for change negotiating on a cheerful first-name basis.

Finally, there are the cases where others do not initiate interaction. Sabonjian must take the initiative in personalizing these relationships. The personal letters he sends at election time are individually typed and each is signed by the mayor. Sabonjian asked a real estate developer who arrived in his office as he was finishing the dictation of an off-year aldermanic endorsement letter, to listen to it. "What do you think of it?" he asked the man when he finished reading. "It's awfully long," the developer ventured. "The people of that ward will love a long letter," Sabonjian replied. "It will make them feel important. They aren't busy, and they don't get much mail. A long personal letter from the mayor will be the biggest event of the month." Thus the letters, each a full page of single-spaced paragraphs, were mailed in behalf of the candidate. The alderman's good deeds and loyal service were extolled and his ill-health was explained. In a flowery closing, citizens were asked to join together in electing this faithful man. Together they could provide that bouquet of flowers he needed and show their appreciation for a job well-done.

Sabonjian's campaign advice is always the same—door-to-door canvassing. His assistance to favored candidates consists of personal letters of endorsement and assistance in their canvassing. His view on losers is usually that they didn't cover their ward on foot.

Sabonjian goes to the people in person and through personal acts. There is, however, a second condition which must accompany presence in creating trust. This is related to the psychological component in accessibility. Sabonjian insists that communications from him must not violate the sense of *Gemeinschaft* solidarity he struggles to achieve with the townspeople. This insistence constitutes a paramount criterion for action. Its importance in the eyes of the mayor produced an interesting dispute with a company the city had contracted with for city-wide garbage pick-up.

Among citizens, there was apparently no clarity on the nature of the contract. Persons frequently had their garbage turned down because it included items not covered in the contract or because there was too much of it. They complained to the company and they complained to the mayor. Complaints had become sufficiently costly that both the mayor and the company agreed that citizens ought to be made aware of the contents of the contract. This included its limiting clauses but also the citizens' right to a second pick-up each week. This second pick-up, which would have no size limitation, could be purchased for a small payment to the company.

The mayor and a representative of the disposal service met to draft a suitable letter. The company man had brought a previously drafted letter with him which he proposed to use. The letter was unacceptable to the mayor who thought it sounded distant, technical, legalistic, and bureaucratic. The mayor suggested that the man compose another letter—in plain language that would refer, for example, to "two cans" instead of "sixty gallons" of garbage. The man pointed out the importance of using the technically correct term since some cans hold twenty and some hold thirty gallons of garbage. The entire contents of the letter posed similar problems. The company wanted their customers to have, from the administration which had agreed to the contract, an absolutely explicit legal statement regarding the exact nature of the contract. Sabonjian would not sign unless other non-legalistic language could be used. Moreover, he wanted the optional nature of the service to be emphasized and he insisted that the same letter inform citizens of free city-supplied alternatives—e.g. personal delivery to the landfill. A sentence suggested by Sabonjian which was acceptable to the company representative was the following:

> The new service is purely optional. If you want an additional pick-up, and are willing to pay $3.00 a month to the company, it is entirely up to you. If you don't want it, just forget it.

The mayor and the company could not come to terms, however, regarding the remaining technical language. Neither side gave in. Eighteen months have passed. Garbage complaints continue but concern the mayor, who explains the contract problem personally to dissatisfied persons, less than did the negative consequences he feared from the letter.

Sabonjian's strategies of personalizing would presumably lose effectiveness as city size made it impossible to reach a sizeable part of the electorate. What can one do with petty favors and personal response? Apparently more than one would think possible. In a town of sixty-five thousand persons one would certainly not guess that all of the factory-employed parents of a class of unselected grade school children would have had indirect contact with the mayor through their children's visit to his office, and half of them would have had some form of direct contact such that their children knew it. Nor would one expect that in the same town, twenty-one out of twenty-six children in another class (whose parents were professional or self-employed) would report communication between the mayor and their parents. If such contacts or the votes which accompany each of the 450 summer jobs can be seen as cumulative, the result over time might be surprising. If three votes could be expected for each summer job, that activity alone could produce a voting block 12,500 strong in ten years. It is not unreasonable to think that this in fact occurs. In dealing with a very loose, unorganized body of voters, even when quite large, one gesture may be enough to so personalize the political order as to create a lasting loyalty.

There are, of course, ways to accommodate increasing scale. Daley adapts this method to a larger political system by using precinct captains. By dividing the labor needed to maintain trust based on accessibility and response at the individual level, he is able to maintain a system based on personal contact. Contact is made at the personal level but clearly identified with the Daley machine. What Jane Addams said of machine politics in 1902 is still telling. Banfield quotes her in the following passage from *City Politics*.

> Many voters, indeed, seem to have valued the turkeys and hods of coal mainly as tokens of friendship, and accordingly of the humanity and goodness of the "organization" and its "boss." Jane Addams, the settlement house worker, explained this long ago: "On the whole the gifts and favors are taken quite simply as evidence of genuine loving kindness. The alderman is really elected because he is a good friend and neighbor."[44]

In an effort to cast this tint on politics, Daley directs his workers to make personal contact. At various campaign rallies in the last few years he has made the following statements.

We will continue to carry the message as the early Christians did—by word of mouth.[45]

No poll can equal the day-to-day visits of the men and women of the Democratic party.[46]

Return to the fundamentals of politics—sell our story door to door.[47]

In Waukegan, such two-step allegiance describes only the relationship between the mayor and members of the Puerto Rican community. An important aspect of this relationship is the blurring of gratitude. The higher source gets credit from beneficiaries both directly and through the Puerto Rican leader who acts as intermediary. In a letter to the mayor, a Puerto Rican in need of legal aid expressed his inability to separate the two either in terms of their responsibility or his gratitude. The letter began "Dear Sir" but was followed by "Bob." After explaining the problem, the writer reassured the mayor with "Eddy Montano [Puerto Rican leader] is going to explain you all about it."

A second response to increasing scale is to continue to emphasize personal concern and official accessibility but without personal contact. This method relies on demonstration of concern for groups with which the individual presumably identifies (hopefully this includes the city itself). Here the politician attempts to demonstrate his concern for the individual by demonstrating concern generally or concern with others like the individual. The mass media becomes the vehicle for portrayal of concern and accessibility. Newspaper examples of informal, amusing, or especially human aspects of Waukegan's mayor and council were discussed earlier as assets in creating trust. John Lindsay's walks through black ghettos seem to have been efforts to elicit trust. The strategy is to elicit trust in one's personal concern through symbolic demonstration and through accessibility of image—if not of person. Sabonjian thinks Lindsay succeeded in winning trust but failed to use it in controlling other officials and personnel. Thus it did not prove a resource in producing where a government must produce—housekeeping demands. Sabonjian remarked early in 1969 when the New York garbage strike was still a fresh issue:

People don't want to blame Lindsay. It's the guys they never see that get heckled. The politicians who only come out in the election years are open to trouble because it's the only chance people get to complain. They figure this is their only chance to heckle this guy they never see except when he's running for office. But people don't want to blame Lindsay. He's had his troubles for a long time but at least he's available. He's out there with the people, he's in the ghetto. He's at the ethnic festivals and the church baseball games. People can believe he cares.

Where Lindsay made his mistake is not to play it up bigger. He ought to attack his council—like Truman attacked his Congress. Truman said they were the biggest bunch of lazy beligerent, do-nothings he'd ever seen. Lindsay ought to say "The reason your garbage isn't picked up is that you've got a bunch of petty politicians for aldermen. Look at the budget they voted for Wagner. Look what they vote now. These guys aren't concerned about *you*."

Sabonjian was not willing to grant symbolic presence the sufficient strength this discussion might imply. Speaking again of Lindsay, he said:

Don't underrate the number of places he does appear personally. Boy that guy makes a heck of a lot of those small time festivals and celebrations that other politicians think they haven't got time for. Lindsay could squash that council. *He's* the guy people know. Not their alderman.

Whether Sabonjian's ideas on New York politics are accurate or not, they probably say much about Sabonjian and successful politics in Waukegan. Sabonjian identifies openly with Lindsay's style of relating to constituents. People must know you. They must believe you are accessible. They must believe you are concerned with an irrevocable concern. They must trust that you have their (and not your own) best interests upper-most in mind. They must believe the possibility of deceit to be nearly zero. If this kind of trust can be created, the politician can act without the constraints of constant supervision, and he has resources from which he may hope to control the structure through which programs are produced.

Trust in Value Representation   A second type of trust is awarded to a person who is felt to represent important values. One trusts persons who are "like" oneself (or what one values) to act in one's behalf. Power is delegated because of identities which are assumed to be determinative of policies. Leader and follower may be united by common social characteristics (ethnic, religious, occupational, regional) or by shared perspectives (allegiances, beliefs, norms, or goals). Power may be delegated to persons who embody an individual's values whether or not he personally embodies them.

This notion of representativeness assumes *natural* representativeness based on ascriptive characteristics (ethnicity, place of birth), or upon non-negotiable conviction. The source of the value identity is thought to be "internal" to the individual—as opposed to being prescribed by the political party or the requirements of election. Trust arises in response to what is accepted as adequate demonstration that the leader is in fact an unequivocal representative of important values.

Sabonjian is most apt to seek this type of trust in dealings with moderately autonomous persons. The notion that persons or groups trust commonality over disparity in selecting leaders assumes on the part of the persons or groups in question a more sophisticated conception of the political process than does primary trust. At a minimum, this conception incorporates an awareness of value conflict and interest representation. The awareness of difference makes possible the identification of one's significant values and of the persons who embody or share them. Identification of persons with particularistic values focuses and defines the areas of group interest for the would-be leader and it signals appropriate response.

Trust in identification of a politician with values in the population is useful to the extent that the population from which the politician seeks support is homogeneous. One would expect claims of representativeness, then, only where such factors as social rank, ethnicity, and life style are constant for the many persons in the constituency or where agreement on norms and goals is high among them. If the community is heterogeneous, these kinds of identifications are damaging to any particular politician who is apt to share characteristics or convictions with only a small portion of the community. The negative effects of identifications which produce trust along very divisive grounds accounts for the distaste American politicians have registered with regard to ideological politics.

In the absence of homogeneity of social characteristics or wide issue consensus, attempts to acquire this kind of trust will appear as broad identifications (Americanism) and bland, platitudinous, general proposals (more city planning). That is, politicians will advertise commonality or congruence with the lowest common denominator or the majority characteristic (or value). Hence Sabonjian's main programs were city beautification, the shopping mall, and the civic center. He refused to take positions on controversial issues (such as school integration and urban renewal) where he feared he might appear to be "working for" a minority.

The corollary propositions which emerge regarding representation are: (1) The politician will make appeals to the lowest common denominator in the value system of the community (the more heterogeneous the community, the more general the appeal) or to values which, while specific, are unimportant or uncontroversial; (2) The politician will avoid value appeal when the issue is defined at a level of generality where values conflict. The latter proposition implies that a neutral position will be recognized as valid and will not be equated with opposition. It may not inspire trust but neither will it inspire distrust. This argument suggests, that is, that opposing groups will have some awareness of political competition. While they may seek to elect persons who are specifically representative of their values, they will nevertheless acknowledge a neutral position. This assumption was certainly implicit in Sabonjian's statement regarding his union-management negotiations.

Dahl's discussion of Mayor Lee suggests characteristics which Lee thought would elicit trust from the constituency.

> In a city where rancor between town and gown is never far below the surface, the Mayor's Yale associations could have been a severe handicap, but his political opponents found it difficult to change the image that Lee himself carefully cultivated of a local boy in the mayor's office, a home-grown Irishman, a family man, a devoted Catholic, a hard-working mayor and a friend to everyone in the city.[48]

Mayor Sabonjian's job is more difficult. His appeal to Armenianism would have a very small audience. For him, direct appeals to this characteristic or to other narrow qualities of commonality would be more divisive than unifying. They do nevertheless occur on occasions where the audience is homogeneous and the mayor's appeal is not apt to have any particular implications for future action. He capitalizes on associational trust when he does not feel groups with alternative values will interpret it as partisanship.

While the mayor would not propose special city funding for Armenian housing, he golfs at the Armenian Open Championship, accepts graciously the Armenian of the Year Award, locates jobs for Armenian teens, assists with problems of Armenian immigration, and speaks at Armenian Night. The interesting fact here is that these activities do not differ from the assistance and recognition Sabonjian accords any of the various ethnic, religious, neighborhood, or interest groups in the community. It is possible, however, for the Armenians to impute what they want to the mayor's actions (to his friendly welcome, to his ethnic jokes). They seem to have a capacity for imputing considerably more than is necessarily implied. When, however, there arises a question as to the possibility of preferential treatment to Armenian applicants for city posts, the mayor is cautious and disclaiming. Observations that a small Armenian population had contributed both a city collector and a building inspector to the city government caused some eyebrow raising. The charges could not find sufficient support, however, to suggest unethical policies. The mayor had noticeably included Armenians but had carefully avoided excessive enthusiasm in appointing them.

With regard to other commonalities, the mayor has similarly avoided narrow associations. Even with regard to his small business background and his Protestant religion—values with fairly common currency—he has avoided identification except in communication with persons narrowly identified with particular values and in statements free of policy implications. His business advice, for example, may be prefaced with "I was in business, you know." His conversations with south siders are frequently dominated by references to the location of their homes, their common neighbors, the fact that they grew up together. Although less so in the later periods of this study's observation than in the earlier, changes in Sabonjian's language and style of speech would make it possible to identify the class or ethnic status of persons to whom he was speaking. Once again, the mayor's statements and manner seem to imply far less identification (more often an attempt to personalize the relationship) than those who wish a value realized are willing to impute. Armenian clients are considerably more insistent in their claims that Bobby is one of their countrymen than is Bobby; south siders tell how Bobby is one of them; small businessmen like to see the mayor as a necessarily partisan official.

All of these groups (or at least some members of each) impute to the mayor far more of their desired positions than can accurately be attributed to him. The willingness of the persons identified with values to interpret his behavior as referring to them, provides the mayor with a resource in attaining this type of trust. Just as factual ethnicity may be assumed to be binding, behavior which is friendly may be read as partisan by those who evaluate and behave in terms of the particular values. This trust, then, may be gained without any hypocrisy other than an awareness of the mis-apprehension of others. The orientations of others may be used as a resource, strengthened by the mayor's sometimes high status and his chief-of-staff or ceremonial function. Using the latter two resources to appeal to the first, he may imply but not act on com-monality. He may, by simply joining fraternal orders or other groups, acquire brothers who impute to him their feelings—what-ever the actual strength of his identification.

One widely held value in Waukegan is home-ownership, in-cluding the rights of property and neighborhood. There are no survey data which can be used as direct support for this assertion and indirect measures are flawed as to comparability and date. Nevertheless, what is available suggests some measure of support. The 1960 Census of Housing reports that 57.3 percent of occu-pied housing units in Waukegan were owner-occupied. Over 58 percent of the total number of housing units were single family detached dwellings. Forty-three percent of the units occupied by non-white families were owner-occupied at that time. These rates seem fairly high by comparison with Chicago, where the figure for total units showed 34.3 percent owner-occupied or with suburban Evanston, where the figure was 43.4 percent.

On an issue such as home-ownership where there is wide con-sensus, Sabonjian can take a firm issue position and still reach a fairly common denominator. He is both praised and criticized for the extreme force with which he proclaims the positions he does embrace. Assuming, however, that the politician's stand re-flects wide feeling, force and apparent commitment would be expected to produce overall gains in value trust.

Many of Sabonjian's firm statements relate to protection of pri-vate property. Cited earlier were his remarks on the necessity of protecting the rights of the home-owners in the area to be con-demned by the state for the lakefront highway. He was quoted in the newspaper as saying: "I keep telling them, 'Don't do anything because there will be demolition in the future: I don't know if you're going to be reimbursed for this kind of remodeling for your homes'" (5-15-67). It is likely that this statement on homes and home-ownership had a much larger audience than the half dozen home-owners specifically involved and it included persons identified in very few other ways with those in question.

The tree-planting program for city beautification was also directed at home-owners, who were urged to buy trees at discount prices. Those which were to be planted in the parkway would be planted by the city. Planting elsewhere in the yard was to be done by the property-owners themselves.

What other values have general currency? Children and parenthood are obvious choices. A main job thrust is summer jobs for youth. He attends regularly the high school athletic and fund-raising events, junior league games, and grade school programs. His enthusiasm for the drag strip was phrased in terms of "Listen, you know I'm all for the kids" (4-3-69). The beach pavillion was set up for youth recreation. Sabonjian told a parent group seeking a skywalk for school children: "I know your kids are just as important to you as the Little Fort students are (with the skywalk). I'm a parent too" (4-19-67). While the generality of appeal in a statement like "I'm a parent too," cannot be denied, its general currency is its weakness. A public figure must exhibit concern for children to maintain parity with other officials. The trouble with the very obvious shared values is that they frequently fail to distinguish the candidate in terms of trust. His only hope is to appear in some way more convincing than others who will inevitably expouse the same position.

Sabonjian perhaps does distinguish himself. He set up a summer program for mentally retarded children and has in helping youth service organizations extended himself beyond what would be expected of a public official. Two letters to the editor suggest this is true.

Allendale School takes this opportunity to thank Mayor Sabonjian for his continuing interest in young people. On numerous occasions he has demonstrated his affection for kids, and we are gratified to find this type of man in public office.

In September while visiting on Allendale Day, Mayor Sabonjian observed a decrepit barber chair used in giving our boys haircuts.

In less than two weeks, Allendale boys were receiving haircuts in a new chair. . . . (2-8-69)

I should like to say that Mayor Sabonjian's concern for children is widespread and always generous. Anyone . . . who has a child with a need is likely to turn up at the mayor's door and he doesn't get sent away. (2-21-69)

Another popular issue is law and order, an issue Sabonjian embraces and expounds. His dramatic response to street disturbances (scarcely riots) on Waukegan's south side brought him national publicity in 1966. He verbally attacked lawbreakers and the judicial system for its lax treatment of them.

In the above examples, Sabonjian's actions do not seem contrived. Yet, it is easy to believe that the mayor avoids expounding on those issues about which his views diverge from those he perceives in the public. Certainly he is not simply engaging in expressive behavior but is well aware of the political impact of alternative positions. His remark on the strike which tied up communications in Chicago in the months preceding the 1968 Convention is suggestive. Referring to the great inconvenience, Sabonjian said to a friend: "I don't know why Daley doesn't lower the boom. Given half a chance I'd land all over the telephone company. Nobody ever lost any votes for laying into a big utility."

There are many values, of course, which do not give way to a common denominator. When divergent values cannot be blurred, overlooked, subsumed, or de-fused, the mayor has alternative ways of taking them into account. These range from a "something for everybody" position to one of complete neutrality.

In the case of the executive, these alternatives may be defined in terms of either the executive's personal characteristics or those of his associates, his total administration.

Dahl's description of Mayor Lee suggests the first type of allocation was important to his personal image. Mayor Lee apparently balanced familial-ethnic-religious identifications and university-popular policies in recruiting support from his Irish-Catholic, working-class constituency and from Yale liberals. Banfield reports that a similar balancing was important in the career of Raymond M. Hilliard as director of the Cook County Welfare Department, and that of Alvin E. Rose as Commissioner of the Chicago Welfare Department. Banfield's statement refers to relations with political actors rather than image with constituents.

Hilliard and Rose had each taken on a coloration likely to insure the maintenance of their organizations in the environment in which they operated. This was an environment in which a variety of interests had to be placated or checked. Hilliard's organization would have been open to attack if, in addition to being a Republican, he had been Protestant, tax-minded, and anti-Negro. As it was, having an Irish grin and being a good Catholic brought him friends in the heavily Irish-Catholic political elite of the central city, and his outspoken advocacy of the "liberal" line in welfare matters got him support from social workers and others who seldom found themselves allied with Republicans. Likewise, Rose, who held a key position in a Democratic Administration which was dominated by Irish Catholics and who was an Irish Catholic himself, would have been in an exposed position had he been closely identified with the "liberals," race-relations reformers, and "spenders" who had been close to the Democratic party since the New Deal. Just as Hilliard needed support from among the natural opponents of a Republican, so Rose needed it from among the natural opponents of a Democrat. What he had to say about "the relief mess . . . commonly referred to as our Welfare State" disarmed the tax-savers in the suburbs who otherwise would have viewed him and his organization with profound distrust. His remarks about Puerto Ricans and Negroes also won him some support from "reactionaries." These remarks were misinterpreted, of course—Rose himself was not prejudiced, and he did not like those who were—but if he had seen fit to do so, he could have phrased what he had to say so that there would have been no possibility of misinterpretation.[50]

These descriptions suggest ways in which achieved statuses may be used to balance or at least blur the presumed meanings of ascriptive statuses. (In the above examples, party as well as ethnicity is assumed to be an ascriptive quality.) Sabonjian was a poor boy and a south sider elected as a Democrat by south side ethnics and blacks. The newspaper opposed his first campaign. He lost no time, however, in making known his willingness to work with money, with industry, and with established institutions. Some feel that his original election hinged on the north side support which resulted from his south side campaigning for school board candidates sponsored by influential north side families. At any rate, he took advantage of his office in making known his interest in cooperation. It became clear that Sabonjian's south side origins were not determinative for his policy positions, that his support from the south side was not ideologically grounded, and that, indeed, his ability to gain support from the formerly disconnected south side was useful in achieving goals which political division had made impossible.

The creation of partial aspect images occurs in several ways. It may be possible to identify a "newspaper public" which gets its image of a public figure from that media and distinguish this group from an ethnic population which accepts the portraits drawn by group leaders. When information sources do not overlap, the separateness of the image aspects presented to groups may remain intact. Another strategy which may elicit from constituents a trust in the existence of shared values is to present apparent proof. The woman who called Sabonjian to praise the beautiful flowers which the city had planted on the boulevard opposite her home was confident that she and Bob Sabonjian shared the same ideas on neighborhood and beautification. Sabonjian's quick response to clients no doubt seeps, in the form of relayed images, deep into the body of constituents. A specific response is apt to be reported through friendship channels to persons who would desire roughly the same service. Sympathy or identity can be imputed to the mayor. Responses, on the other hand, which would suggest unfamiliar or undesirable values are not as apt to be reported.

In some cases, it may be impossible to give something to everybody—at least something important. If primary values conflict, and secondary values are unimportant by comparison, the politician's best strategy is likely to be a complete neutrality with regard to the primary values. He cannot in such cases offer compensating values. He can, however, opt out altogether and in so doing avoid the distrust from opponents which would accompany a partisan identification. Armenianism, for example, (like south side origin, or small business background) is a useful identification only when it is not seen as relevant or contrary to other value systems. When it appears an inappropriate criterion, as for policy decisions, it is best avoided.

The second way an executive may take divisive values into account is through the inclusion of the various value positions not in his personal image but in the composition of his administrative network. Although he is personally non-committal, his staff and board appointees include representatives of various values. Speaking of his school board appointments, Sabonjian said:

> I attempt to pick honest and fair grade school board members who represent the community groups such as Catholics, Negroes, Latin Americans, and the business community. I try to have two women on the board. (3-13-69)

That board during this study has represented a good sample of ethnic and religious groups, the business community (as the mayor pointed out), good government activists, and progressive elements associated with the League of Women Voters and liberal Jewish factions.

Theodore Lowi, in his study of mayoral appointments in New York City, discusses the process of balancing various values in the distribution of appointed posts:

> Values, traditional and new, are the currency of political transactions. The bid for party or group influence on the Mayor's decisions is made in terms of these and related attributes. But values are inseparable from the personnel who bear them. In the process of claiming representation for their values, groups must offer persons or types as candidates for appointment.[51]

Lowi is, in this passage, viewing mayoral appointments from the viewpoint of organized groups (parties or interest groups) engaged in competitive politics. Groups vie for representation when they cannot achieve greater control over outcome. Lowi feels that, in New York, organization is the only way views will reach the mayor and find representation in his administration.

In Waukegan, the mayor does not rely so narrowly on the definitions imposed by organization. He makes it his business to know the city and to be aware of its value composition; no goal has higher priority or receives more time. His determination to possess an accurate map is an important reason for his wide circulation in the community, his open-door office policy, and his placement and rewarding of informants.

James Coke has suggested that the reliance of politicians on organized groups for expressions of public opinion is characteristic of larger rather than smaller metropolitan areas.[52] It may also be that organized interest groups relay information regarding the policy orientations of dispersed persons (organized by abstract values rather than neighborhood) in the way that precinct captains are able to relay information regarding neighborhood and ethnic sentiment. In this sense they would supplement rather than replace a territorial map (if this latter existed). At any rate, Mayor Sabonjian and Mayor Lee (as indicated by his use of the sample survey) seek the views of the unorganized. Sabonjian's appointments represent a total city view rather than any clear identification with organized interests. Nevertheless the values represented by appointed individuals are usually quite apparent. On the school board, for example, there is a black south side barber. While he does not represent any organized group, Sabonjian feels he is a good spokesman of south side black opinion. His barber shop is centrally located for both haircuts and gossip.

Such appointments serve multiple functions for a mayor faced with a community where value conflicts often cannot be resolved. By appointing leaders of organized groups, he may coopt them and thereby discourage potential opposition. When this is not possible, he has nevertheless exempted himself from responsibility. Speaking with a black representative of the Chicago Council on Human Relations, who charged that the school curriculum was not adequate for the needs of black children, Sabonjian replied:

> . . . . [Black representative] voted for it. . . . . [Second black representative] did. What can I do? If they won't represent the people, how can I? I'm the mayor.

Had these men not voted for it, the mayor would, nevertheless, have had a backstop. As he said to the black committee which requested more black representatives:

> There's no doubt that integration [of the schools] is inevitable but I can't pack the court, so to speak, in order to hurry it along. All groups must be represented. I'm looking at Negroes as individuals but they're still an ethnic group. . . . I've got to have a balance or I'll have one group or another up in arms.

Whether organized special interest groups provide the representatives or not, the existence of value representation on boards and staff contributes to the image of the administration consequently created among elements in the public which adhere to particular values. Appointees of different races, neighborhoods, and beliefs return evenings from their jobs to homes scattered throughout the city. To their friends and neighbors these persons no doubt suggest an image of the city government. The administration includes people like themselves. In making the constituency aware of city appointments and hiring, the newspaper serves, like the appointees themselves, to create an image out of composite data.

In the handling of appointed posts and boards, there is a movement between "something for everybody" and strict neutrality which is analagous to the handling of the politician's personal image. Again, this is a matter of emphasis. When conflict is low, the mayor may stress to those whose values were not subsumed by over-arching values that their particularistic values are represented. If the represented groups focus on a single non-divisable value and accept no substitutes, he, once again, opts out of the conflict. In this case, he renounces any ability to act. Interestingly, the only instances where this observer saw Sabonjian take a hands-off position with regard to appointees was the school board. Sabonjian's consistent position has been that this board, once appointed, is out of his control or influence. "I never interfere with the school board." School issues are probably avoided for the same reasons as was urban renewal. They are frequently and logically controversial—given the necessity of financing by referendum and the likelihood of wide attention to matters of policy.

Because value trust is associated with special interests, it is, in communities where the population is heterogeneous, an asset of uncertain worth. Because it is directly related to the desire of persons to see a value position realized, it is difficult to acquire on a broad scale and difficult to sustain. It frequently suffers from the same type of problems as exchange politics with interest groups and the policy-oriented forces of good government. Although this analysis of value trust included groups united by a self-conscious social identity with groups united by interest, the problems common to exchange and trust are most often associated with the population of moderately autonomous persons identified by commonality of interest. Because these persons focus on problems with specific implications for action (i.e. issues or rights), they are more troublesome than ethnic partisans. The desires of the latter group are not by definition translated into action imperatives and only on occasion are they actually translated. The value trust which is useful to politicians is that which is not accompanied by assumptions about action implied. Unlike good government or organized pressure group values, where the value is itself a political goal (social, ethnic regional, racial, and religious), identifications may yield trust which is unrelated to specific goals for or expectations regarding government action. When a group with a common social identity does translate that identification into a goal, it has acquired the character of the issue-oriented groups and should be considered as such. It is also likely that interest definition will be accompanied by organization and that the organized group will have acquired greater autonomy along with the new focus.

Trust in Role Adequacy Trust in role adequacy is the most external of the three types. It is conferred on a politician who, it is believed, has achieved or is achieving what can be rationally expected or required of him in a given position. This trust assumes an understanding of the capabilities and the restraints of a particular office; it assumes an evaluation of absolute results in terms of rational precepts. Unlike primary trust which results from a particular type of human bond, or value representation which indicates a consciousness of kind and an identification with commonality, this type of trust assumes no attraction to or identification with a particular individual or group. Its prototype carrier would be the rational economic man of the utilitarian philosophers.

Behind the notion of rational behavior is a trust that the system will operate satisfactorily for the purposes of the individual or the group if the system's roles are played adequately. When trust is likely to rest on this type of evaluation, therefore, the politician's job becomes that of convincing persons that he accepts the instituted context and is adequate to the determined role. He attempts to demonstrate his willingness and his ability to realize the potential of the role without violating its limits, show his willingness and capacity to discharge the designated duties of office or political logic, effect the purposes of the system and, in general, play well his role in the political scenario.

What persons would be apt to make role adequacy the evaluative criterion in political life? Logically, it would be those persons who feel that the present form of political organization is advantageous (or adequate) for achievement of their goals or who feel, at least, that no other realistic form would be superior. This perspective is apt to be associated with autonomy as it was defined in terms of resource independence, alternatives, and choice.

Persons with independent power bases may assume that a role

actor will be responsive to opportunities for resource maximization and threats to system maintenance. Their positions in the social structure give them the wherewithal to appeal to the rational man in the politician. They are apt both to understand the rules of the game and to have the resources necessary for effective action in it. So long as the politician behaves "rationally," their success in achieving goals is apt to be high. So long as the politician follows the dictates of understood role logic, he is calculable.

In the case of the primary relationship, the politician's particularistic orientation is assumed to have priority over the "rational" decision. In the case of the value bond, the abstract value is thought to be the determining loyalty. In the case of the role actor, the role is central. An understanding of the particular role pressures will make the behavior of the incumbent predictable because his behavior is role-determined. "Friend' and "representative" are, of course, roles which have implications for action and are predictable if so defined. Neither is synonymous with the role "mayor," however. The fact that the particular class or group structure of a community may produce situations where one of these roles is more or less conterminous with that of mayor should not becloud this point. Behavior which is role-determined refers to behavior, which in terms of the specific role (in this case that of the mayor), is expedential with regard to the opportunities and constraints of the role.

In the concept "expedentiality," I include two foci: 1) The politician will be politic. He will be receptive to arguments based on reason, mutual self-interest, the public good. 2) The politician will be political. He will respond to pressure formulated out of game logic and applied at points where he and opponents know he is vulnerable.

The politician who can be counted on to be politic—prudent and technically competent—will be open to reason and persuasion. The *Tribune* editor who remarked that "Any mayor would be soft in the head not to want an improvement like that [McCormick Place Exposition Center] for his city," assumed politic behavior. Persons with independent resource bases are often in good positions to appeal to this type of reasoning, since interrelationships among the institutional sectors which confer their powers are usually pervasive. They are apt to share goals with the mayor, for, like him, these men have occupations which force their attention to the level of the larger unit. Their overview of the city may well include attention to its social composition, its resources, its employment structure, its population transiency, its housing, its tax base, its public facilities and its opportunities for education or training.

In the spring of 1966, eighteen "influentials" named twelve issues as the most pressing problems facing Waukegan. Eight persons named the revitalization of downtown, six mentioned the need for an industrial highway, six mentioned a desire for a junior college, five mentioned the labor shortage, and five named school finance.

As of 1969, the downtown area has a modern complex of government buildings—city (including the new library) and county. Streets have been altered to handle more traffic, demolition has removed many of the city's unsightly structures, and numerous parking lots provide ample parking space. The construction of the government complex and city cooperation in programs for parking lots and traffic movement have been important boosts to the extensive private renovation carried out by area businesses. There is now an industrial highway and a junior college (although the mayor did not participate directly in the realization of the latter goal). Sabonjian's determined program to expand moderate-income housing is explicitly directed to the shortage of adequate housing for industrial workers. Given these factual results, the persons who stated above goals as pressing would probably feel that in terms of absolute results institutional cooperation was adequate.

Eight of these city influentials, though not questioned about the mayor, nevertheless volunteered comments on him. The executives of the two largest industries in the area were among them, and they focused on the same point. One industrialist stated:

> The mayor has done a great job in uniting the community, pulling it together, generating enthusiasm. The mayor helps those who help themselves. Really gets things done that way. He was responsible for the courthouse, the city building, the library, the off-street parking. We couldn't get mobilized for anything until he came into office.

The other industrialist cited city disunity as the most pressing problem in Waukegan, but described it in structural terms and acknowledged Sabonjian's role in fighting it:

There's a lack of cohesiveness here. It's hard to get things done. People are divided by ethnic boundaries, by class, by race, by neighborhood, and by occupation. Sabonjian's been a real force in overcoming this. He personifies cohesiveness but can't really accomplish it. It's much better than before, of course. But we need more unity. We can't get together on low-cost housing, school financing. . . .

Persons oriented to long range predictions, general tendencies and absolute results would be less swayed by specific statements or personal appeals. Presumably their focus would be on the effect they expected the county complex or a downtown convention hall to have on downtown development, or the effect they expected moderate-income housing to have on the worker shortage, on the balanced city budget, or on the achieved goals like the industrial highway and the continuation of bus service.

They would not be concerned about a newspaper article which reported that the mayor thinks industries "ought to put their money where their mouth is," and goes on to say:

It's disappointing when the industry here cries that there is no labor market and here are ready made workers for them [college students seeking summer jobs] who would appreciate the jobs.

They make the excuse that they hire the children of their own employees first and therefore nothing is available. I don't believe them. (6-10-69)

There is little chance that such ravings would receive much attention from persons whose evaluations were phrased in terms of structural change, long-term goals, past and projected programs. "The Mayor is kind of a bull in a china shop," remarked the newspaper publisher. In common with the mayor, these men have occupations which provide them with an overview of the city which is apt to include an awareness of the tenuous interrelations among institutions and factions, the complexity of goals like stability, integration, or prosperity, the conflict among groups, and the potential for immobilization.

Industrialists who read that Sabonjian has attacked area industries would counter this datum with the well-considered view that "Sabonjian is good for industry." Given this belief, they could assume that some purpose other than hostility motivated the act. One might discount it. Or one might ask if it meant that Sabonjian's office security is jeopardized by his inability to produce summer jobs, and if so, industry ought perhaps to produce jobs in order that Sabonjian stay in office. If it is simply the mayor's way of eliciting identification and support from the young, the unemployed or the working class, the strategy is tactical for the purposes of industry too. "We can work with Sabonjian and he can work with the town."

An industrialist who had been one of the major contributors in the installation of an expensive lakefront lighting system told of it with great pleasure. Sabonjian, he said, had heard there might be hoodlum riots on the beach and was afraid the industry buildings might be damaged. But the mayor had felt that a lighting system would deter such actions. In spite of the cost to himself and other industrialists, this executive was delighted. It was a great advantage, he said, to have a mayor who could talk to both sides, who knew what was going on and could stop trouble before it got out of hand.

It is perhaps safe to assume that persons in New Haven who analyzed politics in terms of role pressures would, so long as he continued to produce according to their objective standards, be sympathetic to the problems which prompted Mayor Lee to portray himself as local boy and a home-grown Irishman, a family man and a devoted Catholic.

The influentials were by no means uniformly positive in their remarks about the mayor. Nevertheless, their responses seemed to indicate role evaluation and gradients of trust. One man objected to the mayor's rough language and extremist statements. But he did not assume an ideological position with regard to them. "A mayor can't talk the way he does," this man remarked. "He ought to have a hatchet man." A second influential had a different reason for concern. "He gets things done, but he has more power than is normal or right. I realize the need to get organized but I'm suspicious of so much power in one man." The man who made this remark was personally committed to civil rights action. The mayor, he felt, did not represent his value objectives. In tactical terms, he understood quite well why the mayor behaved as he did. It is possible, however, to be simultaneously committed to a minority goal and to understand the positions and the problems of an elected official. With regard to the issue that concerned him, this man had not been able to persuade the mayor of ultimate benefit. Nor had he the tools or the know-how to muster an offensive capable of forcing a change in the mayor's behavior. This brings up the second aspect of role trust—trust that the actor will be political.

The politician who is political can be counted on to play the political game in a rational, predictable fashion. When a politician can be trusted to respond to events in these terms, it becomes possible to calculate the strategies which might bring desired goals within reach. Although groups interested in change are rarely able to combine factors so as to play a fully satisfying winning game, the possibility exists so long as politicians are playing a game the rules of which can be known. Thus Representative Lowenstein expressed role trust in Lyndon Johnson when he launched five thousand students onto New Hampshire streets to bring out a vote for Eugene McCarthy. Lowenstein did not expect the actual result which was the president's withdrawal from presidential competition. He believed, however, that Lyndon Johnson would be unable to ignore a strong protest vote against administrative policies. Because Johnson was assumed to be a role actor, activists assumed that he could not ignore a significant register of constituent opposition. (Eugene McCarthy, on the other hand, elicited value trust. *Had* he responded to pro-war demonstrations, his following would have withdrawn its faith in him. Indeed the very suggestion, in post-convention months, that he had betrayed the cause in his senate voting brought disillusionment among followers who insisted upon uncalculating, forthright statements of commitment.)

V. O. Key is speaking of role adequacy in the following quote about Bibb Graves of Alabama:

> Unencumbered by ideological fixations, he impressed local politicians over the state as a practical man who could and would do business with them to meet the immediate practical problems of governing with mutually beneficial results.
>
> In campaigning he guided himself by the advice of his local friends. His speeches began with generalizations but soon got down to specifics: the ten-mile stretch of road in the county over which a crow couldn't fly. . . .[53]

Local examples of strategies which incorporated appeals to expedentiality can be seen in the efforts of various special interest groups. Advantages accompany the ability of community leaders to supply investments large enough to assure program success and maximize output from city endeavors. The newspaper publisher has a good notion of the price he must pay for city cooperation, of the forces he knows to constrain mayoral action, and the compromises he must be ready to accept if the mayor is to be cooperative. He is apt to frame his proposal so as to incorporate the mayor's pressures. This was true, for example, in the publisher's drive to acquire the Standard Metropolitan Statistical Area designation. Various facets of the designation were investigated so as to locate those which would appeal to the mayor. Such factors as the role of publicity and the allocation of credit were no doubt considered. If the proposal could be made desirable in terms of the mayor's game, the mayor could be trusted to behave in a predictable ("rational," "reasonable," "sensible") fashion; the publisher could hope to achieve his goals.

The proponents of urban renewal also attempted to incorporate what they felt were the pressures which might inhibit executive action. Businessmen invested a large portion of their budget in newspaper publicity; members of the League of Women Voters arranged for a community workshop and neighborhood teas in an effort to solicit the support of the public. Had these efforts been successful in eliciting popular support, the mayor and council might have been more receptive to the maximizing opportunities provided by the bill. The nature of perceived political imperatives might have been changed.

Dahl would not be talking about persons interested in role adequacy when he notes that in America, "the virtues of amateurism are so highly regarded that leaders whose major occupation and source of income is politics often try to disguise the fact in order to avoid the epithet 'professional politician.' "[54] On the contrary, to those who know how to play the game and have the resources to play effectively, the "pro" is the man with whom they can deal, the man they trust to behave predictably, the man who will respond to their plays.

The number of persons identified as being community leaders was small. The inactive persons who correspond to them in terms of autonomy were also few. Among these persons, relations with the mayor are infrequent. Few interchanges occurred during this period of observation; thus the conclusions regarding community leaders are based primarily on interviews with them. Theories on high autonomy constituents are still more speculative. Such persons may prefer the use of private means to clientele politics as a way of securing desired ends. The incidents which suggested this were the cases where wealthy residents chose to protect their neighborhood through private purchase of property rather than attempts to influence the mayor or organize pressure upon the council.

There seem, however, to be logical hypotheses which are implied in the model used here. One would expect that upper-class persons who dissociated themselves from active influence would, nevertheless, have an interest in certain outcomes, structural changes, and long-range performance. Some of these persons have large investments in the area. This group could be assumed to share the interests of their active counterparts. Persons with substantial commitments in the area might remain inactive only so long as they felt that their institutional interests were being anticipated and protected. In this sense, they might evaluate the chief executive as one would evaluate a city manager. One would be interested in his ability, his training, his efficiency, his professional and political skills.

Persons without major commitments would probably be interested in the area as it compared with alternatives. What are the visible results of this administration? What are the costs—social, economic, esthetic? How predictable is the system? How safe is the community? How often is it necessary to do privately what might be expected of the city?

High autonomy constituents might be expected to concern themselves with the following types of reports, whether the alternative to approval would be action or withdrawal: (1) the bi-annual budget reports (the tax rate, the bonding, the indebtedness, the distribution of funds), the balance between budget and product, i.e. the cost of residence. (2) the school finance reports (tax sources, distribution of funds between various programs and teachers' salaries). (3) statements volunteered by Sabonjian comparing Waukegan's budget with that of other cities (4) newspaper reports on Sabonjian's aggressive fight in the state legislature over a bill proposing a change in the distribution of the sales tax revenue. [This lucrative tax now benefits the retail centers which collect it, Waukegan among them. Sabonjian was swift in launching his opposition to a bill which would change it. To fight the bill proposed by the Lake County Republican Senator and Majority whip, Sabonjian took with him to Springfield others of the area's most influential Republicans, its foremost economic dominants, and a newspaper executive. "You're penalizing the cities that are progressive," he charged, "and you're favoring the bedroom cities." (3-67)]

In appealing to role trust, the politician will attempt to demonstrate through the media and through observable results, that predictable, desirable, efficient "progress" is achieved under his administration. He will avoid involvements which might suggest (by his participation, or by the results of his action) that he is incompetent, impractical, unprofessional, or unpredictable (e.g. ideological, irrational, utopian). Programs will be controlled and predictable. They will include visible public improvements and social advances insofar as these are extensions of existing institutions.

This type of trust may become increasingly important in a general sense as the scale of the political community grows larger. In large-scale communities primary trust would be a function of identification of the political head with his subleader intermediaries or his press image. Inevitably each would have some independent effect upon his presentation to the public, although he has opportunities for control over that presentation in terms of his organizational control and his use of the press. In either case, it would be difficult to establish a primary quality in an indirect relationship.

With increasing scale the possibilities for effective value representation, except at the most general level, would be similarly diminished as the various publics received the same image. This problem could be diminished to some degree through use of competing communications channels (intermediaries, press).

Trust in role adequacy, however, would be fostered by increasing scale since scale separates persons with varying commitments and varying powers, increases the complexity of their interlocking jobs and requires that they have performance standards and summary measures (the Dow-Jones average, the unemployment rate, the GNP, the war dead).

TYPES OF POLITICAL BEHAVIOR AND TYPES OF TRUST

Thus three types of trust may be elicited by a political executive—trust in a primary relationship, trust in value representation, and trust in role adequacy. All three may be seen as expressions of relationships which are distinguished by degree of interpersonal involvement. Primary trust is associated with a relationship which is perceived as personal. Value realization suggests a supra-personal bond. Role adequacy describes an impersonal evaluation. Sabonjian works to build trust in himself as (1) a human being who is a primary reference figure—often a primary associate, (2) a representative embodying ideal values, and (3) a skillful role actor.

These types of political trust bear a problematic relationship with the categorizations of mayoral commitments proposed earlier. These accommodated pressures included subleaders, pressure groups, community leaders, the following, the good government voters, and the upper-class indifferents. The political behavior associated with various commitments was seen as a function of relative autonomy (resource independence, alternatives, and choice) and type of participation in the political process.

While these two typologies (of structural relations and of trust) are analytically distinct, their different dimensions seem related to the degree that it becomes possible to discuss a preponderance of one or another type of trust among particular categories of persons. Autonomy seems to have a bearing upon the mode of trust which will be predominant. Persons with few independent resources (subleaders, following) were seen as most apt to seek goals through political means, to become political dependents and to return compliance and support for benefaction. Persons (pressure groups, good government voters) whose jobs and investments outside the political sphere confer a degree of independence but who nevertheless feel that they have intersts which can be advanced or protected only by local government constitute a second category. Persons (community leaders, upper-class indifferents) who control resources of major institutional importance constitute a third category. Resource strength enables these persons to achieve private goals without recourse to political action. Institutional goals normally require cooperation among the various leaders (including the mayor), but goals are sufficiently related to make cooperation often desirable.

Although there is no necessary correlation between autonomy and occupation, education, and income, it is empirically true that access to these latter resources is strongly correlated with the existence of choice. These variables are predictive not only of structural position and factual choice but of intellectual range as well. Insofar as autonomy is associated with occupation, education, and income (as opposed to decreased interest in rewards), it seems to be associated also with particular modes of trust. It is the existence of intellectual scope which is important in determining the mode of trust which will predominate.

Persons whose worlds are limited both feel and are more vulnerable than persons with greater resources. It is difficult for such persons to supply the links or understand the process which connects the individual with the larger structures. They are accustomed to person-to-person relations and are most prone to trust relationships which can be evaluated in this way. Persons whose focus is on the group or the neighborhood have a somewhat expanded sphere of interest and knowledge. The individual may feel more independent by virtue of his group membership, his occupational skill, or his home investment, but his values must compete for favor with those of other groups controlling similar resources. Individuals whose occupation, income or education require or enable them to view events from a broad institutional perspective are apt to see job and neighborhood as results of complex forces. Insofar as this is true they trust a man who appears adequate to a job which must stabilize and should benefit a variety of essential commitments.

The paramount criterion for determining autonomy, however, was the availability of alternatives, the existence of choice. The correlation between autonomy in this sense and the socio-economic variables which determine intellectual scope is imperfect. Nor does intellectual scope require a rational evaluation of role as against a personal or value response. The Chicago Republican who hated to oppose Dan Ryan because Ryan meant well was not responding in terms of objective results, but in terms of personal affiliation. The Waukegan influential who rejected Sabonjian's stand on racial issues placed values, although qualified by sympathy with position, over role action. Nor is there a purity in the responses of other individuals. The Puerto Ricans in Waukegan seem torn between a primary trust in Sabonjian himself and a powerful identification with the organized ethnic community. One suspects that the lower level politicians who counted on Bibb Graves' practical politics also viewed him as something at a patròn (Key calls them a "personal following"). It seems then, that there is considerable room for variation within the over-arching congruence of typologies: variation in terms of individual deviant cases and variation in terms of mixed cases. In many instances also, the three types of trust are simultaneously present; the correct differentiating factor may be the amount or significance of each type in any particular relationship.

The mayor centralizes power through the manipulation of resources. He becomes powerful as he accumulates control over them. The mayor justifies power by establishing himself as the legitimate person to hold office. In seeking and receiving trust, he creates his mandate.

NOTES

[1] Blau, p. 94.

[2] In Dahl's sample of registered voters in New Haven, 57 percent gave an unqualified "no" to the question, "If you had a son just getting out of school, would you like him to go into politics as a life work?" Only 28 percent gave an unqualified "yes." *Who Governs*, p. 179.

[3] Arnold Rose, *The Power Structure* (Oxford University Press, 1967), p. 80.

[4] Dahl, "The Analysis of Influence in Local Communities," p. 37.

[5] Norton Long, *The Polity* (Rand McNally, 1962), p. 27.

[6] Banfield, *Political Influence*, pp. 259–69, fn. 344–242.

[7] Parsons, p. 48.

[8] *Ibid.*

[9] *Ibid.*, p. 49.

[10] Banfield, *Political Influence*, pp. 243–4.

[11] *Ibid.*, pp. 245–6.

[12] *Ibid.*, p. 277. See 276–85 for Banfield's discussion.

[13] Dahl, *Who Governs*, p. 89.

[14] *Ibid.*, p. 96.

[15] *Ibid.*, p. 105.

[16] *Ibid.*, p. 133.

[17] Machiavelli quoted in Lasswell and Kaplan, p. 273.

[18] Banfield, *Political Influence*, p. 271.

[19] Dahl, *Who Governs*, Chapter 28.

[20] Lasswell and Kaplan, p. 156.

[21] George Homans, *Human Group* (Harcourt, Brace and World, 1950), p. 427.

[22] *Ibid.*, p. 426.

[23] *Ibid.*, p. 425.

[24] Moses, pp. 39–40 (emphasis added).

[25] Greer, *Last Man In*, p. 71.

[26] Rose, p. 77.

[27] Moses, p. 40.

[28] Parsons, p. 49.

[29] Sebastian de Grazia, *The Political Community* (Phoenix, 1963; first published 1948), p. ix.

[30] *Ibid.*, p. xvii.

[31] *Ibid.*, p. 73.

[32] *Ibid.*, p. 75.

[33] Lasswell and Kaplan, p. 136.

[34] Scott Greer, *The Emerging City* (Free Press, 1962).

[35] *Chicago Tribune*, 3-24-67.

[36] Sabonjian decided the city ought to have a flag, arranged for it to be designed, woven, and dedicated to the city.

[37] *New York Times*, 3-28-68.

[38] *Holiday*, 12-63.

[39] *Time*, 3-15-63.

[40] Moses, pp. 28–29.

[41] Banfield and Wilson, p. 110.

[42] Banfield, *Political Influence*, p. 118.

[43] *Ibid.*, p. 108.

[44] Banfield, *Ciy Politics*, p. 118.

[45] *Chicago Tribune*, 2-11-65.

[46] *Chicago Sun-Times*, 3-21-67.

[47] *Chicago Daily News*, 10-2-68.

[48] Dahl, *Who Governs*, p. 119.

[49] *Chicago Daily News*, 8-11-66.

[50] Banfield, *Political Influence*, pp. 65–6.

[51] Theodore J. Lowi, *At the Pleasure of the Mayor* (Free Press, 1964), p. 8.

[52] James Coke discusses the effects of city size on the development of voluntary organizations as intermediaries between citizens and government officials. In smaller cities, he says, cases are handled in a more particularistic way. Problem-focusing organizations are endemic to larger cities only. Coke, "The Lesser Metropolitan Areas of Illinois," *Illinois Government*, no. 15, November, 1962, published by the Institute of Government and Public Affairs, University of Illinois.

[53] Key, pp. 51–2.

[54] Dahl, *Who Governs*, p. 990.

6

Summary and General Parameters

The Mayor's Mandate is a study of the role of the political head in a heterogeneous community. A political head is a person who has no superior to whom he is responsible, but one who is subject to community recall. The analysis of this role is formulated with regard to the activities of the mayor in a diversified midwestern city of sixty-five thousand. The city is divided by economic interests, ethnicity, religion, race, and political tradition. Yet the present mayor has been able to expand his one-time minority following into a broad community coalition. In addition, he is credited with enormous power and organizational effectiveness.

This study obviates problems of biased selection of issues and discontinuity in their study by supplementing issues analyses and in-depth interviews with extensive and continuous participant observation. The result is an analytic frame which is not restricted to the visible and dramatic aspects of political action but extends to the web of relationships, existing over time, within which power is created and maintained.

The role of the political head is described in terms of his commitments to six population categories. These are derived from crossing two variables: political autonomy and political participation. The mayor is committed to groups which occupy different positions in the socio-economic structure of the community, wield different types of power, make different types of demands, and experience different levels of awareness. Responsibility to these various groups limits the mayor's alternatives.

At the same time, the political head uses community diversity as a resource in acquiring political power. He may use the lack of integration which exists in both the private relations in the community (economic and social spheres) and in its public organization as a resource in achieving political power.

He uses his position (its formal powers, its visibility) or simply

187

his personal energy as a base from which to facilitate cooperation among population groups which are interdependent but not co-ordinated. He exploits those situations where interests converge but information, awareness, and communication do not. He brings together buyers and sellers, employers and employees, those who want to give and those who want to receive. As coordinator, rather than supplier, he builds personal power at relatively low cost to himself. The web-like integration of complementary goals in the private sphere may be termed horizontal integration.

By facilitating the ability of persons or groups to achieve individual goals, the political head acquires control which then makes it possible for him to facilitate the achievement of collective goals, and, so doing, to acquire further power. He can use the power he has accumulated in horizontal integration to require the various groups in the community to participate in the realization of a collective goal. The organization of the community in pursuit of a collective goal may be termed vertical integration.

A continuing danger exists in the possibility of contradiction arising among commitments. If definitions which emphasize conflict rather than complementarity of interest become prominent, the mayor will be immobilized. Since he must maintain stable relationships on a fairly short time schedule, the mayor will shy away from broad controversy. If he must act on controversial issues, he will seek to control the scale and timing of the unpopular actions. He will try through early negotiation and control over presentation to impose his definitions on proposals he receives. For personal sponsorship, he selects programs with multiple payoffs.

Personal power is thus associated with the politician's ability to create additional resources. His basic resource is incomplete integration or "slack" in the community, i.e. groups with complementary goals are inadequately integrated with one another or the low integration of the community as a whole prevents the attainment of collective goals. The political entrepreneur turns symbiotic parts into a functioning political unit, first by politicizing the symbiotic relationships (extracting the political component for himself) and second by producing the possibility of collective action. Coordination increases the productiveness of available resources. Personal power is created out of the new surplus. It is the entrepreneur's payoff for his repudiation of the zero-sum game and his faith in the "game against Nature."

As described, the political enterprise is intimately related to characteristics of the community without which it could not be expected to work. *It is necessary that differentiated but interdependent social segments lack complete organizational integration.* The accumulation of power by a political entrepreneur could not occur in a community where there was little differentiation and nearly complete organizational integration. This situation is associated with the ideal-type primitive community.

Differentiated but interdependent parts might exist within an institutional area or specific organization as in the case of employers and employees. Differentiated parts may also be the institutional areas themselves. One could cite cases where electoral approval of economic proposals depended, for example, upon the solidarity of religious or ethnic groups. The re-integration of the religious or ethnic segments with the economic or the governmental is the job of the political entrepreneur.

A homogeneous community within a complex society would lack such differentiation. There would be no need within the community for horizontal integration. Its members, by whatever criteria homogeneity is established, would constitute a category of "likes" for which exchange complements must exist elsewhere. An ethnic group (homogeneous in terms of job opportunities, political connections, or whatever) must be organized in terms of outside structures. A homogeneous residential community could presumably be organized in the same fashion if it were possible for the would-be leader to operate in terms of complementary institutions and persons located outside the community. Organization which is not zero-sum must occur in terms of complementary interests. The greater the number of variables along which members of a community are homogeneous, the less is the opportunity for horizontal organization within it. The politician, of course, would have some part in defining the degree to which possible complements were identifi d.

It is possible that a community whose members are not horizontally interdependent might, by virtue of their common fate, be vertically interdependent and desire vertical integration. Vertical integration would not in such cases grow out of horizontal integration. The entrepreneurial model would be only partially relevant.

Since there would exist no ongoing structure of more or less coercive power, verticle organization in homogeneous communities would be apt to be *ad hoc,* issue-related, and transient. Activation would last as long as the common "problem." Organizers would use ideology or appeals to past performance in organizing the group for collective goal attainment. Appeals of the latter type would constitute a variation on the entrepreneurial model.

The slack which makes entrepreneurial centralization of influence possible requires that, in addition to differentiation and interdependence, there be inadequate integration. This requirement assumes two conditions. The first is that differentiation be accompanied by position-related interests or values which, being position-related, can be achieved through coordination. Differentiation is a source of social energy only if self-conscious interests exist or can be created. A population, even though interdependent in terms of some goals, would not be a source of social energy if individuals or groups rejected either the goals of integration or the integration itself. A totally satisfied population could not be mobilized in terms of goals. Traditional or extremely conservative societies might approach this variation as might societies where notions of justice coordinate exactly what individuals have with what they feel they should have. Efforts to coordinate the categories "employer" and "employee" would be similarly meaningless if unemployed persons refused for religious or ideological reasons to see employment as a means to financial welfare or employers refused to see the available personnel as eligible for employment.

The second condition related to the integration of differentiated parts is the requirement that existing integration be inadequate. In a completely centralized system there would be no "slack." This situation is approximated in the totalitarian state wherein all aspects of social life are presumably directed by the central government. It is approached to the degree that in any system coordination of various activities becomes centralized. Other things being equal, there would be less political slack in a one-industry town than in a multi-industry town. There would be less slack in a community with only one church than in a community with many churches. There would be less slack in a community where the actions of a single church and those of a single industry were coordinated with one another than in a community where this was not true. There would be less slack *within* bureaucratic structures than among them; at the top levels, where internal order ends and external interactions take place, integration is inherently problematic.

In America slack may be greater than elsewhere for sacred authority is relatively minimal or grounded in the market principle and organizational pluralism is dogma. In other societies, the entrepreneur may encounter a greater degree of cultural, ideological or religious resistance or greater organizational closure. The American sense of private interests may contribute also to the ease with which power can be garnered from horizontal integration. These qualifiers suggest the following addition to the original proposition regarding the system within which the proposed model for power centralization would hold. *Ideology, tradition, law, or existing organization must not make the coordination of complements either inevitable or impossible. Political slack exists when integration is desirable to many, and possible, but not automatic.*

There are further conditions which could be expected to decrease the amount of slack in the system. One would be a scarcity of basic resources as in the case of an economic depression. The fewer the resources available, the fewer which can be obtained and redistributed by the political entrepreneur. Moreover, his obtaining a benefit is apt under these circumstances to cost him in terms of zero-sum exchange. Opportunities for multiple payoffs would be reduced. The politician might still coordinate and redistribute, but his chances of producing in very many cases would be smaller and integration more costly.

One would also expect changes in the scale of the political unit to affect this model of power. As the size of the unit increased, it would become increasingly difficult for a political head to personally organize the components of the system. Possibilities of intellectual comprehension diminish along with the possibilities for personal communication. As scale increases, the political head's communication with constituent parts would become more reliant upon organizational intermediaries or upon the public media. As this occurs, each of these groups increases its power at the expense of that held by the political head, for some organizational slippage is inevitable. Information received may be inadequate or incorrect. Persons receiving benefits may associate the benefaction with the intermediary as well as or instead of the political head, diluting or removing the payoff for the latter. Others may compete for the loyalty of the intermediaries. Those in possession of the means of communication (both the organizational intermediaries and the press) may sabotage the messages which the political head sends and receives.

Insofar as a political head becomes a "public" rather than a personal figure, i.e. as the politician is forced to rely more and more heavily on the media in reaching his public, there is the additional probability that any given public self will be presented to more publics than intended. It would be more difficult to be simultaneously for labor and for management in public than in private statements. If all statements are to reach all publics, the dangers of apparent hypocrisy increase. What might look like complementary needs to a political executive, could be defined by community interests as zero-sum positions. To the degree that the media defined action this way, the politician would be limited in his proposals for horizontal as well as vertical integration to what he perceived as widely acceptable values.

If media have negative effects upon the redistributive powers of a political head (horizontal integration), it is by way of another variable: political trust. *Behind the ability of the entrepreneur to achieve integration among differentiated, symbiotic but not sympathetically organized parts, is the need for trust in the man who provides the link.* The population categories which together constitute the basis for the political community do not trust the intentions of the others. Their definition of the game, the "political formula," is zero-sum competition among antagonistic parts. Nor do these parts trust the would-be organizer of action—the politician. The creation of trust involves appeals to several possible perspectives which provide frames for evaluating trustworthiness. These are (1) *trust in a primary relation*, (2) *trust in value representation*, (3) *trust in role adequacy*. Each is time consuming.

Trust in a primary relationship indicates the kind of trust associated with *Gemeinschaft* society, with family and friendship. It is a personal relationship expressed in terms of accessibility, concern, sympathy, solidarity. Trust in value representation derives from a consciousness of kind. Social, value, or interest identities are assumed to exist. Power is delegated because of commonalities which are assumed to be determinative of policies. Trust in role adequacy assumes that behavior will be expediential in terms of the opportunities and constraints of a given role within a complex role system. Because behavior is role determined, it is predictable. It allows one to anticipate and to take into account the probable reaction of the other in response to possible developments. Primary trust is a personal relationship, a human bond. Trust in value representativeness is a supra-personal bond which requires a notion of differentiation and subgroup identification. Role adequacy is an impersonal evaluation of competence; trust is placed in an actor's ability to discharge a particular role in a predictable fashion.

The political head elicits trust in himself through appealing to the various frames which persons use in evaluating trustworthiness. *These frames of trust are distributed differentially in the population; the distribution may be related to autonomy.* Primary trust is perhaps the dominant mode among low autonomy persons, trust in value representation may be most common among moderately autonomous persons; trust in role adequacy seems located most often in the attitudes of the very autonomous.

Such are the circumstances of the mayoralty and a strong mayor's adjustment to them. The story is one of a mayor who insists that the means of government serve the ends of government. As he sees it, government is primarily the pursuit of collective goals and not primarily a process for determining them. This position distinguishes him from his more legalistic predecessor. Critics of local government divide similarly between those who emphasize output and those who emphasize constitutional propriety. Those of the first persuasion measure government against criteria such as the infant mortality rate, the unemployment rate, the standard household income. Their critical theme is inaction, or ineffectuality. Those of the second persuasion look for evidence that an office holder stays within the legally defined rights and duties of his position. They delight in exposing corruption of means or usurpation of power.

In the interest of generalizability, I have underscored the character of action politics rather than the particular ends of action. Yet, of course, these ends have been sub-themes organizing much of the political process in Waukegan. They, in turn, would seem to result from an interaction between the mayor and his constituencies. The mayor works within the rules by which a community pursues goals. He works as leader in this pursuit, but within a structure; his world view is similar to that of various constituencies.

The lower autonomy sector of the constituency exerts a constant pressure on the mayor to provide jobs, decent and reasonably priced housing, safe and good neighborhoods. Middle-class constituents press for order, service, and recreational facilities. Both of these groups look to Waukegan to provide opportunities for their children's adulthood and for their own old age. Constituents with the greatest autonomy seek dependable and efficient city government, economic growth and social stability.

These priorities however dovetail with Sabonjian's own values. He has lived through the range of situations from poor boy to small businessman to political head. His origins were with the poor and the ethnic; he reached working age in the depths of the depression and with an ethnic handicap. In 1971, he told a college audience that he was totally committed to his program for low and moderate income housing. Opposition to this program was rooted in prejudice against ethnics and blacks. "I can remember" the mayor boomed, "when there were lots of neighborhoods in Waukegan that I couldn't live in because of the color of my complexion." The existence of opportunities for the hardworking is basic to Sabonjian's notion of the proper polity; appropriate pricing and payroll are his mechanisms. Housing at the right price should be attainable regardless of the color of complexion. So grows the housing in Waukegan. The corollary of Sabonjian's commitment to the availability of housing opportunities is his commitment to the creation of ever widening job opportunities. The major reason for his commitment to growth is this enthusiasm for an expanding job market which, needing workers, creates opportunity for advancement within it.

Sabonjian describes Waukegan as a place where most of its present citizens were born and where many will die. This is, of course, true of the mayor himself. Only in recent years, after a huge swing through the social structure, has he considered leaving Waukegan. His local patriotism, his concern for the aged and his plans for the future are those of someone dedicated to a particular city not only in its present but as a place for one's old age and for one's children and grandchildren. Hence his observation that "The economy is changing. The children of blue-collar workers aren't blue collar anymore" resulted in active and successful re-cruitment of the growth industries to employ those white collar children. Housing for senior citizens repays parents and holds together Waukegan families.

While Sabonjian's most intense loyalties are with those seeking entry, he understands the middle-class interest in service and city beauty. Both of these have been priorities of his administration. But such things as pollution control are not (in his Waukegan) to be paid for by the poor. Industries which are "paying their way" in terms of good jobs have his sympathy over middle-class enthusiasm for clean air.

The civic elite's concern for efficiency and dependability in city government poses no problem to a mayor who is deeply committed personally and organizationally to predictability of behavior and speedy achievement of goals. With respect to goals, the conver-gence of values between this elite and the mayor is largely a matter of mutual commitment to stable growth. For persons with heavy economic and institutional commitments in an area, this goal sum-marizes a host of considerations. Major institutional plans or pre-dictions require at least minimal assumptions about the future of the community. Positive planning requires the assumption of future well-being. Sharing this orientation, the mayor and these community figures find points of agreement in purpose that over-ride disagreement and define points of cooperation.

Sabonjian works well with those whose jobs require predictions about the future because his image of Waukegan is completely future-oriented. The past for him was a time of poverty and ex-clusion. There was in it, however, the promise of future inclusion, economic improvement, full citizenship, personal and group advancement.

His vision of future Waukegan is definitely social; Waukegan is a place where the lot of its citizens—especially the underdogs—improves with time. The mayor is not attached to the city of the past, the old downtown of the city's history, or the neighborhoods of his youth. He has helped downtown merchants and older fac-tories to update their facilities and has worked to update older neighborhoods, but preservation does not interest him. He has pursued a policy of annexation which has dramatically changed the shape and size of the city. "Evanston fixed its boundaries" he says of a nearby city. "It was too good for Skokie back when they could have annexed. Now Skokie is the economic center and Evanston is dying." Thus Sabonjian incorporated the western developments, providing for the entry into the city of new opportunity structures and new tax sources. Competition should occur within and not against Waukegan.

Sabonjian has a very local view of Waukegan, but no intention of missing larger trends. He is committed to the survival of Waukegan as a community of opportunity. And as opportunity changes, so must Waukegan change.

1 2 3 4 5 6 7 8 9–BC-79 78 77 76 75 74